U-TURN
"The Teenage Turnaround"

A Full-Circle Mentoring Guide for Parents and Young Adults

Terence B. Lester

U-Turn "The Teenage Turnaround"
© 2007 by Terence B. Lester

Scripture quotations marked KJV are taken from the King James Version.

Scripture taken from the Holy Bible, New International Version®. Copyright © 1973, 1978, 1984 International Bible Society. Used by permission of Zondervan. All rights reserved.

Scripture quotations marked NKJV™ are taken from the New King James Version®. Copyright © 1982 by Thomas Nelson, Inc. Used by permission. All rights reserved.

ISBN: 978-1-59916-409-0

Printed in the United States of America

DEDICATION

I dedicate this book to my beautiful wife *Cecilia,* who is my best friend and my constant support. With similar passion, I humbly acknowledge my mother, *Connie Walker,* who pushed and encouraged me never to give up. Finally, I'd like to be a source of inspiration to my toddler nephew *Carmelo O'Neal,* who sat and played on the keyboard while I was writing. I believe that he will grow up to become a great man.

ACKNOWLEDGEMENTS

~

My whole being is filled with praise for the many individuals who have blessed my life. Please indulge me as I publicly thank them for what they have done for me:

I dedicate this book first and foremost to **God.** Without Him in my life, none of this would be possible. I love Him for what he's doing in my life, as well as in the world.

Special thanks have been earned by one of the most supportive people in my life, my wife, ***Cecilia L. Lester.*** I want you to know that you are my heart. I love you for who you are and what you bring to our marriage. Your support has been more than the wind beneath my wings. I will never forget these words you shared with me. You said, "Don't let reaching for the future have you too obsessed to find happiness for the moment. Be happy today. Remember, happiness is a choice, and depression is the result of neglecting that choice. While you have your health, don't spend too much time trying to please others; you could rob your own happiness. Happiness doesn't cost anything. Whether you're the richest or the poorest, you have to travel to happiness, you don't arrive there." I love you dearly, Cecilia.

I would like to thank my mother, ***Connie Walker,*** for your never-ending prayers and for never giving up on me. I thank you for pushing me when no one else would. I love you with all my heart. In similar manner, thanks are due to my stepfather, ***Dewitt Walker,*** for coming into my mother's life and providing the love she has so long deserved. You have brought such joy into her existence. I want you to know that I respect you immensely and appreciate the wisdom that you deposit within me each time we talk. You are a great person, and you have been good for both my sister and me.

I would like to thank my sister, ***Ashley Lester.*** I love you and believe in you very much. I believe that you will grow into a wonderful woman. I also want to thank my older sisters, ***Latasha Bradford*** and ***Monica Lester***, along with my four nephews and two nieces. I love you all and am glad that I have you in my life.

I want to say thanks to my Dad, ***Tyrone Lester***, for coaching me as a child and for showing that it is okay to take risks when it comes to dreams. You have encouraged me to go above and beyond. Our best days as father and son are before us.

To both sets of grandparents, ***Gloria and Carlton York and Jessica and Herman Lester***, I love you for always being there for me and for the foundation that you've laid for me. You have been great examples. I love you all with all my heart.

I'd like to thank **Denise Burns** (Cecilia's mother), for raising a beautiful young lady who ultimately became my wife. You have embraced me as your son. Along with Ms. Burns, I must thank **Cherise and Frank Moss**, Cecilia's aunt and uncle, and **Shavonne Garrett,** her godmother. Our marriage and relationship are stronger because of the love that all of you have shown to us. Thanks so much.

I have been blessed with loving support from **Pearl and John Bland** and **Susie Burns,** my wife's grandparents, for welcoming me into your family and feeding me delicious food. You are now my grandparents too. I count it all joy to be so favored.

To the Easons, **Ron and Marie**, who have both been angels in my life. You have been like a second set of parents. I love you and thank God for you.

I am grateful to **Bishop Dale C. Bronner, Sr.**, my pastor and spiritual covering, for writing my foreword and believing in me. You have been a great role model in my life, and I have learned a lot from you. I love you and will teach others what you have taught me.

Jerry and Jada White, I thank you for showing me what great faith is. I love both of you.

I would like to also thank **Sharia West**, my favorite teacher who pushed me to achieve, along with your husband, **Kevin West,** who has become a big brother to me.

I would like to acknowledge **Isaac Walters.** Ike, you will go very far in life. Thanks for being a brother to me and having my back. I would also like to give a special thanks to: **Erik Moore and family, Jeremy Smith and family, Elliott Jackson and family, Harvey Strickland and family**, and **Octavious Felton and family**. I thank you all for being like brothers to me. I would like to thank **Jason and Pearilya Thomas** for being good friends to my wife and me. We love you both.

I would like to thank **Dr. Joe Martin,** my favorite professor at ABC for being one of my favorite teachers and mentoring me in ministry. I would like to thank **Uncle Frank** for supporting me, giving me wise advice, and listening to me. I love you like family. Likewise, I would like to express appreciation to **Martez Spearman** for being my "play" nephew and one of the sharpest young men that I've ever seen. You will go far in life.

I want to thank **Marquis L. Phelps** for being a brother from another mother. You are one of the sharpest men I've ever met. Your character alone is a treasure in itself. I believe that you and **Dalina** will go very far in life.

Table of Contents

Part 4: WHAT'S STOPPING YOU?

FOREWORD

~

The largest room in the world is the room for improvement. In this book, Terence Lester becomes transparent by creating an anthology of a remarkable change that transpired in his life. One will clearly see that change is a process, not an event.

Our mistakes and failures teach us much more than our successes. Failure isn't fatal, so we can't let what we have done define who we are! Our history has no power to stop our destiny. Henry Ford said, "Failure is the opportunity to begin again, more intelligently." Through the multiplicity of experiences Terence has had, he uniquely motivates others to believe that anyone can change, no matter how hopeless they have been. His inspiring story, coupled with practical information, will help anyone transform his or her life. Even though we cannot turn back the hands of the clock, we can certainly wind it up again!

Only a fool does the same thing over and over and expects a different outcome. So if we want something we've never had, we must be willing to do something we've never done. I have watched Terence grow over the past few years. He has come a long way and has overcome a lot of obstacles. His heart now is to help prevent others from making many of the mistakes he made and to show a way out to those who are entrenched in wrong habit patterns. The power of prayer along with God's grace and mercy create the turning point for lives that need a new beginning! With God, all things are possible!

Terence has learned how to be a good student; now he has become a good teacher. So get ready to experience an exciting journey that will teach you many valuable life lessons and set you on a path for optimal living!

Bishop Dale C. Bronner, D. Min.
Senior Pastor and Author
Word of Faith Family Worship Cathedral
Atlanta, GA

INTRODUCTION

~

You have probably heard someone say that another individual has made a one hundred and eighty degree (180°) turn. People use this phrase to describe a big change in direction or behavior. It might mean that someone changed for the better, but sometimes it means that their behavior became worse. If you really were thinking about making a positive change, it would be better to think about going "full circle" or three hundred and sixty (360°) degrees mentally. Turning your life halfway around is not the same as turning full circle. By going full circle one has the opportunity to start all over again.

It is not by accident or chance that you have received this program or mentoring guide. Someone thought enough of you to want to introduce a better "game plan" for your life. They thought so much of you that they made a move to help you to develop or change your way of thinking and begin to approach some of the things that you must face. They wanted to make sure that they did their part to help to prevent life from throwing "salt into your game."

If you really want to be successful, it is necessary to run the full race 360° in order to make lifelong mental changes that will help you. Let's look at an example: have you known or heard of a drug addict who kept fighting to be free of drugs? If you take a drug addict out of his normal surroundings for three months, he might make a few changes for a little while. But if after that time he starts to do the same thing all over again, then the process was never complete. This is why so many addicts try over and over to stop using drugs. They fail to become drug-free simply because only the environment changed. The mindset remained the same.

Think about the earth as it rotates on its axis. A rotation of only (180°) would leave half of the earth in darkness all of the time and the other half in daylight. This does not reflect balance nor does it allow for a full 24-hour day with the benefit of both sunlight and darkness. Would you want to live in a world that is all day and no night? Do you want to live in a world that is all night and no day? There are places such as Alaska, for example, where there are long periods of darkness and very little sunlight. If you live in the sunny southern places like Georgia, Florida, South Carolina, Alabama and other southern locations, you have grown accustomed to plenty of sunlight. Living in darkness would be a great adjustment for you. It would take a minute. You would miss the more familiar balance of sunlight and darkness.

Finally, I recognize the importance of this balance and want to share its value with as many young people as possible. There are many "experts" out there who have studied a lot of books and who have gone through many schools. They used the information from their studies along with statistics and became authorities on many of the situations that you face presently. In many instances, they have provided excellent information. On the other hand, there are others who have *lived* through most of what they have written and studied about. This book is written about many of those experiences. There have been some episodes in my life that I would not like to live over again. In the chapters that you are about to read, I will go over a few of the things that I have gone through and overcome. I believe that if I can share some of these experiences with you, maybe you won't have to go through them, or you might at least handle them differently. It might help you to know a little about my life.

BEEN THERE, DONE THAT

Chapter 1

First Two, Then One

~

"At the end of the day, whoever supports you, be grateful."
~Terence B. Lester

Many young people are born into a family with two parents living together in the same house. Later, for a number of reasons, things might begin to happen, leaving only one parent in the actual household. In the African American community today, almost seventy-five percent of all children in the community are born into single-parent households. If you find yourself in this category, don't let it get the best of you. Don't walk around with a cloud over your head hating the world. There are thousands of other kids that have walked in your shoes who lived to tell wonderful stories about how they made wonderful lemonade from bitter lemons. They found a way to sweeten Kool-Aid without sugar. In other words, they were determined that, even though they wanted and needed the love and presence of both parents in the home, they would manage to survive in spite of it all. I was one of those kids who had two parents at home at first and later found myself being raised by only one—my mother.

The whole deal seemed so unfair. My parents separated when I was really young. I was hurt and did not know how to handle my family's falling apart. It made me angry that they couldn't just keep things like they were in the beginning.

Growing up in a single-parent household presented a bunch of options. I had the choice to either: (a) raise myself and teach myself to be a man, (b) let my friends raise me, or (c) try everything "out there" and learn from my mistakes. I tried all three of these. Trust me, it wasn't easy. My life was a real mess. Talk about confusing. Sometimes I did not know which way was up or which way was down. I lost contact with what was good and what was bad. I floated between doing things that made sense and things that were absolutely foolish. I had a good mind and the ability to think. I just had trouble using these God-given gifts the right way.

I tried everything possible to fill the void of not having my dad around. I tried joining a gang. I cut school. I smoked cigarettes. I disrespected teachers and other adults. I got into fights, stole cars, shoplifted in malls, and even managed to get kicked out of middle school. I held in everything that bothered me, especially my mom and dad's breakup. I felt no one understood me. I felt neglected. I began to build a holding cell of negative thoughts, grudges and lack of forgiveness. Eventually it was "me against the world." Let me tell you, feeling like that produced a lot of anger, blame, and hurt.

Now, let's go back to the one parent that I had left in the household. Let me stop right here and share a piece of unsolicited advice. If you have a mom who is encouraging you and doing everything that she can for you while you are in the middle of all the little "messes" that you can find, then stop and think about how much you are hurting her. I hurt my mother with disrespect, and by wasting her money and precious time. I forced her to go against a world that stuck up its nose at me and said, "This child is not going to make it."

I am so glad that, as the world cast its vote against me, she stood solid and said, "Oh yes, he will." There is a reason that players from the NFL and NBA use their brief on-air moments during a game to say hello to their mothers. They remember that even before there was a coach, it took someone else to get them to the playing field or on the court. It often started when their mothers, at great sacrifice, signed them up in a local recreational athletic league. Think about it. A lot of times, these were single mothers who sacrificed time and money to involve their sons in organized sports. They filled their weekends going to games and participating in fundraisers to pay for uniforms and equipment. By the time these athletes make it to professional leagues, it dawns on them that someone paid a special price in order for them to "suit up" on a professional team.

Although it happens less often, there are some dads that have taken on the responsibility of raising a family without the benefit of the mother's being in their life. A recent well-received movie by Tyler Perry painted a picture of just such an example in an African American household. Whether it is your mother or your father who has stepped up to the plate and decided to be there and give you direction, then you should show them love, respect, and appreciation. They are not the enemy. They are a blessing in your life. Believe me, I have not always seen my mother as my guardian angel. Sometimes I felt as though she were on a mission to drive me out of my mind. I am so glad that I lived long enough to know that she is the best friend that I could ever have. She was even my friend when I thought she was dispatched from hell to make my life tough. She is an even better friend today as I thank her for "hanging in there" and for pleading my case during one mess after the other. Believe me, my life was a trip.

Is your mother on your case? Is she screaming her head off? Is she constantly in your business? Does she have some problems with some of your friends? If so, you need to thank her. She cares.

Unfortunately, I can show you some young people who have all the freedom they want, who come and go as they please, and whose parents don't bother even to try to correct them anymore. Why? Because they have literally given up on their own children. My mother NEVER abandoned me. If she had, I am convinced that I would be dead.

I don't want to take all the credit from my father. I was able to see him during my childhood and still see him from time to time to this day. Do we talk everyday like a father and son should? No. But that doesn't stop me from loving him. Since the day I was able to remember and know things, he has been my hero. Although I saw him do things that were not right, I've always looked up to him in a way that I still do today. In spite of feeling a lot of disappointment as a child, I see him as a hero of sorts in my life. He always will be. I hold on to those moments when he proved, in his own way, that he thought enough of me to face life with proper perspective. I have forgiven him for the times his absence caused me pain.

When I was about nine years old, he carried me to a local recreation center to enroll me in football, basketball and baseball. I was really good at all of these sports and probably could have gone far in all three, but I was running with the wrong crowd. My behavior and attitude were all in the way. In spite of his absence, my dad contributed a lot to the leadership skills that I exhibit today. By coaching me in sports, he contributed to my discipline and leadership. He even helped me not to be a coward or allow myself to be bullied.

I remember a day when I had gone up the street to play ball. This older kid started bullying me and pushed me down on the ground. I ran to my grandmother's house in search of my father. When he found out what had happened, he took me back to the boy and made me fight him. What he did was make me confront my fears. That is a life lesson for which I will always give him credit. I am not encouraging you to go out and hit everyone that does you wrong. I don't encourage you to make physical contact, because sometimes it could lead to violence where someone might lose their life. Always think of the big picture before you get into it with someone over something small. But I also know that there are some instances where running away from the things in life (outside of school) can backfire in a big way. Later on in the book, I will share some pointers on conflict resolution. I credit my dad with being my first teacher in this area. Just like every other human being, he might not be perfect, nor is he the President of the United States, but deep down inside he has a good heart. The older I get, the more I learn to respect him. Daily, I learn more about some of the factors that contribute to the frustrations that a man encounters in life.

If you don't see your father very much or even at all, I encourage you to cherish any opportunity to make contact with him and be around him. Life is funny. It really isn't promised that you will have forever to make it right. As I look back at my life, it sure wasn't the Cosby household. But, even when I watched *The Cosby Show* on a weekly basis, I could not help but notice that they had times that made you think and forgive. Even America's model family had a crisis every now and then.

Whether it is your mother or your father as a single parent, don't disrespect the one that stays, that prays, that pays. Also, pray for the one who did not remain with you. Forgiveness is a good thing. It is the key that closes your past and unlocks your future.

If your parents are together and working together to help you, then you are doubly blessed. Respect them both.

Chapter 2

Portrait of a Life Gone Wrong

~

"If someone is going down the wrong road, he doesn't need motivation to speed him up. What he needs is education to turn him around."
~Jim Rohn

As I grew older, I found out that it was more difficult for me to develop into the man I was destined to be without having had a man around to emulate. My middle school years are the best illustration of this difficulty. I tried everything possible to fill the void in my life. At this early age, I found myself kicked out of school on the last day of sixth grade. I held so much pain inside, not knowing that all of these negative emotions could eventually lead to depression, physical illness, stress, violence, and drug abuse. I tried to find ways to fill a void that only total healing and the Creator could fill. Things just got worse as time went on.

The ninth grade was a really tough year for me. I was hurt and did not know how to handle the pain. I got into so much trouble, and, even though I was an intelligent child, I flunked many classes needlessly. I deliberately ran with the wrong people and made a habit of doing the wrong things.

My tenth grade year was not much better than the ninth. I continued to fail classes and get into trouble. I was too far off-track to graduate on time. I was hanging with the "in crowd" -- the so-called popular students. I quickly became known all over the school. I became a follower, willing to do whatever it was that the "in crowd" did. I was searching to fill the empty places in my life. I wanted to fill the lonely places in the cell that I had created out of pain, frustration, and loneliness. I had been building this cell since the day my dad walked out of my life.

By eleventh grade, I was forced to go to an alternative school. I was arrested and had two felony charges against me. On one school day, four of my friends and I decided to cut school. We went to another school, with weapons. Someone told the resource officer and he approached us. With great athletic ability, I ran across the cafeteria, jumped over a rail with Olympic speed and escaped from the school. The officer chased me for a couple of miles and finally gave up the chase. Three of my friends got away in a car. Another was not so quick and was caught immediately on the site. By association, the police linked me to the crime. They returned to my school and went through the yearbook and began to look for me. It took a month for them to pick me up. But that day finally came.

It happened on a Saturday morning. They picked me up and carried me to juvenile detention. As I rode in the police car, it seemed that everything that all of the teachers had predicted for my life was coming true. I was on my way to jail. I was headed for failure. I would never amount to anything. I would never graduate. I was charged with trespassing on school property, fleeing from an officer, and destruction of school property.

They carried me to a very uninviting building and placed me in a tiny cell. They stripped me of everything that I had, including my "pull-out" gold teeth. They also took my nice shoes and socks and gave me an orange jumpsuit. Unfortunately, this was not the last time that I would go to jail. My bail was set around ten thousand dollars each time I was locked up. My mother would have to pay about one thousand dollars of this before I could be released to go home. I became a hero to my peers, while adults looked down on me for acting like a fool. No one came to my rescue -- other than my mother. This is only one incident that I'm telling you of, but I was involved in many other wrong-doings that took me to the adult jail. I am not proud of some things that I have done in the past, because they could have ended my life.

My mother had to go through the pain of seeing me through all kinds of unnecessary trouble and foolishness. At the time, it did not seem like foolishness to me. I had to fight my way through this mean world, a world where my dad was yanked out of my home and left me with a mom who refused to mind her own business. At this point, I was not glad to have her all up in the middle of my business.

However, jail was so bad that I could not eat my food. All I wanted was out of there. I was singing a different song. My mother could meddle in my business as much as she wanted. It was fine with me.

I hope by now you are "feeling me." When I came down the street, people did not think of me as "Terence-the-Good-Fellow." Actually, it was the exact opposite. People saw an angry little terrorist totally out of control. A more proper description would have been "Terence-the-Gangsta."

Have you ever walked down the street and heard car locks clicking as you passed by? Well, that was my world. People decided I was a thug, based upon my open display of anger, my appearance, my language, and my outward show of negative emotion.

As big and as bad as I wanted to be, I never wanted to go to jail. I had begun to set up an identity. It was that of a life gone wrong. My mother continued to fight back on my behalf. She was not willing to allow me to drive myself off an emotional cliff. Is that where your mother is today? Is she fighting for you and pulling you out of all kinds of trouble? Are you pulling away from her and demanding to be free? She might be the very person who saves you from jail, a bullet, or death. The cemetery is full of young, cool brothers and cool sisters who would not listen.

After a while, I realized that all of those friends who thought I was cool never bothered to show up when I was actually in the worst trouble. I was good enough to smoke, drink, and party with. However, not one of them came to the jailhouse to be locked up with me. When it came to jail, it was their time to scatter. It was my time to be alone. No one showed up at my mom's door with money to help get me out of jail. There were no words of encouragement from my "homies."

When I eventually started to turn my life around, they did not find me cool to be around any longer. They walked out of my life. I did see the police officer again, the one that had chased me during that high school cafeteria incident. We actually belong to the same church now. His eyes welled with tears when he saw that I finally got it together. There were so many other guys that he had to lock up who did not make it. Some of them will be in jail until the day that they die. I told him that what he did to me was one of the best things that ever happened to me. It shocked me, deprived me of my freedom, and made me cherish life.

Jail made me feel like an animal. It isn't a place that you would ever want to go. Take it from someone who has been there. It is a stinking and ugly place to end up.

Chapter 3

About to Burst

~

"As soon as you trust yourself, you will know how to live."
~Johann Wolfgang von Goethe

Before I left high school, I had the privilege of coming in contact with a substitute teacher who inspired me to find myself by writing. I had been writing a lot of things down since I was about twelve years old. When I was about fifteen, he convinced me to make it a regular part of my day. He saw it as a way to express my deepest thoughts without having to enter into debate with anyone or be interrupted by opinions or disagreement. For me, it worked. Before that time, sometimes I felt as though I were about to explode.

I began to write down everything that I was going through. Even though I had a lot of trouble going on in my life and in my mind, for some strange reason the negative experiences were transposed into writings that were positive. Even though I was mad as the devil, my writings did not reflect anger or hostility. I ended up going to an alternative school where the principal and counselors all labeled me as a student who would never graduate and suggested that I try to get a G.E. D. They told me that I would never make it. During my teenage years, I had about 25 teachers, principals, and counselors all tell me that I wouldn't make it. I even dropped out of the alternative school. I had gotten really lost, simply trying to find myself. A lot of young brothers who lose themselves will not be this honest, because it hurts so deeply to share. Let me tell you something: don't drop out. I thought so much about getting my G.E.D., until I found out what it was. Before you drop out of school like I did, you might want to know what a G.E.D. is. "G.E.D" stands for, "General Educational Development." It was created around 1942, during World War II. At that time, they developed a test for veterans so that they would have something equal to a high school diploma to help them go to college.

Later, they offered it to non-veteran adults. On the reading test, you only have to have a 9th grade reading level. This test basically says that you are an average person, good enough to learn only so much. If you are in school, you are capable of doing your work. You only have to believe in yourself and find a tutor if you don't understand something. In today's society, it is very hard to land a good job without an education. I ask you please not to settle for a G.E.D, but to hang in there and finish your diploma. My mother disagreed totally with all those people who said I couldn't finish, and that I was nothing but trouble. She kept pushing me forward, even though I wasn't giving her much visible evidence to feed her faith. But I found out later that faith works that way. You don't need evidence. You just need to believe.

My mother and I were struggling through a lot of miscommunication. I felt as though she did not understand me, and she felt like I didn't listen. Isn't it funny that if we "marry" our past hurts, they can cause us to "divorce" our future? I was doing just that. The next year I was scheduled to graduate, but was too far off-track even to think about it. The strange thing is that I continued to write wonderfully positive things while acting like an idiot.

I continued to treat my mother with disrespect and finally got kicked out of the house at seventeen. I lived out of the trunk of my car. I had taken all of my things out of my room and placed them in the car, because I had no other place in which to store them. I lived in my car and with a friend for five months while in school as a fifth-year senior -- unnecessarily, dangerously, foolishly. I had a nice home to live in that was warm and comfortable. Because I was not walking in wisdom, I set myself up to have to live in my automobile. I created my own hell.

This whole experience provided more material about which I could write. How did I get here, and how did it all happen? What good could I pull from it? I encouraged myself on paper.

Perhaps you feel as though you are about to burst. You may feel like banging your fists against the wall until there are holes in it. Maybe you feel that nobody is listening. How many times has it ticked you off that no one is paying you any attention? Do you go through every day wondering why everybody is ignoring you? Once, I lived in that same world. Today, I am free. I am here to say that because I understand that, I will try to make sure that you are free too.

Chapter 4

Enough Finally Became Enough

~

"When a man or woman gets tired of finding dead ends, he or she seeks a detour."

~Terence B. Lester

By now, my graduating class had marched without me. My mother had been deprived of the wonderful experience of sitting in the auditorium looking anxiously for her son to march down the aisle wearing a cap and gown and with a diploma in his hand. She deserved to be one of the proud parents smiling and waving as I walked by; the problem was that I was nowhere to be found in the line. The music played without me.

I'd hurt my mother for the last time. Finally, I just wanted to see her happy. By now I realized that she too was hurt when my Dad walked out of the door. She had been through so very much and I was just causing more pain. So, after my class graduated, I made up my mind to go back to school. Yep, I became a fifth-year senior. I went after dropping out, still holding on to some of the baggage that encouraged failure in my life. I tried to cover up the pain this time by messing with a lot of females. I was having internal battles. Something in me wanted to do so well, but the things I held on to gave me the option or convenience of not caring.

Because I was determined, I got through my senior year and finally graduated. However, I was still depressed and lonely. Guess what? There weren't enough girls in the world to remove the loneliness. That too, was another trick of a determined, deceitful, and wicked enemy.

At eighteen, I tried to commit suicide. In my mind, there was no reason for living, since I could not find out how to be a man. There certainly had to be more to it than messing with as many females as I could attract. I knew that I had taken unfair advantage of them, because, they, like me, were lonely and looking for companionship and approval. I was admitted to a hospital and sent to the thirteenth floor, the Psychiatric Ward. Man, that was an absolute trip.

I started looking at my life and making a list of all the things going wrong; my Mom was finally getting a divorce, I was being blamed for being a bad influence on my sister, school was going bad — everything was going down wrong. I wrote my mom a letter and said that I was going to kill myself. I called my girlfriend and told her what I was about to do. I left the door open for my mom, so that she could get in when she came home. I made a small cut on my wrist. Then I just sat there. The next thing I knew, I heard my mom screaming for me to come out with the police.

They came in and got me and put me in a straight jacket. They carried me out of the house as I looked into my mom's eyes. I saw a terrified woman. I had finally convinced the one person who had held out hope for me, when no one else believed, that I was crazy. They placed me in a truck. My girlfriend and all of the neighbors were all there, just shaking their heads. They drove the truck away as I yelled and screamed and demanded to be released. But they would not listen. But the worse part of the trip was yet to come.

When we got to the hospital, I got a first-hand visual definition of "crazy." I saw all kinds of people engaged in negative behavior. There was one guy jumping rope. The problem was he was busily involved in this activity without a rope. People were carrying on full conversations — with themselves. Very quickly, I knew that this was not where I belonged. I was hurting. I was alone. But I was not crazy.

They were prepared to admit me for a period of sixty days, until they allowed me to sit and speak with a doctor who listened, examined me, and released me that same night. He recognized that I had perfectly good sense. The small cut on my wrist was insignificant. It was nothing. It was my spirit that was bleeding. I left knowing that I had to do things differently. I remembered the eyes of my mom, my girlfriend and the neighbors. They thought that I was too far gone for them to be able to help me.

At the tender age of nineteen I had done it all. I had abused alcohol, smoked cigarettes, and used a lot of pot. It finally became evident to me that it was not my friends, the clothes, the shoes, the cars, or the girls that would make me happy. It was something much deeper than that. During this time of being in the lowest valley of my life, I realized that I had been placed here to help lead thousands of others like me out of a maze of trouble and destruction. I had to walk through this terrible valley so that I could speak from life experience rather than speculation. In other words, I know about the hell that you are going through. I don't have to imagine what it's like.

I want you to know that you are not alone in any way. It just feels that way sometimes. I am still relatively young, but I have gone through enough that now I feel like an authority. Hard and tough times gave me lessons in wisdom, in making choices, and in helping me to share my life with you.

First, I want you to know that you can turn your situation around without the crowd. Remember, I had gotten to the point where I felt I couldn't do it without a lot of other people, who were actually heading in the wrong direction. Then I came to the point where I realized that I could not do it with the crowd. I finally understood that I needed help far greater than they could ever provide. I needed a change. I was so tired of getting into trouble and missing out on life. I remember my mom when she told me to go to church. I thought, "Yeah right, so they can judge me. Church is so lame." But I am a living witness today that finally accepting her advice and getting "plugged into" the church is what saved my life. I could have been dead today, but God had a plan that overruled the plans of the enemy to destroy me.

At age twenty, I returned to church and published my first book of poems. I never forgot the teacher who encouraged me to "get it out of me" and on paper. As I look back over my life, I remember some powerful factors that turned my life around. They are none other than God, His Son Jesus Christ, and a made-up mind. I had to turn my thinking patterns around. Remember, I told you earlier that if you only change your surroundings and not your mindset, it will do you no good.

A slow shift began in my life as I struggled through this experience. Little did I know that I had to nearly go out of my mind to keep from going absolutely crazy. Because I spent a few hours in a place for the "mentally disturbed," I just might be able to help you maintain your sanity and not have to go there yourself. I have been to hell and back. I strongly suggest that you cancel your reservation.

There is a real enemy out there who "comes to steal, kill and destroy." That enemy I'm referring to is what older people call the Devil. But that enemy can also become our own selves hurting our future. Don't let it happen to you. He'll have you jumping without a rope. Or worst of all, you'll have yourself jumping rope without a rope by making choices that could hurt your future. Then he'll stand back and laugh with all of your so-called friends. He'll also laugh when, one by one, your friends leave you all alone.

Chapter 5

Why I Didn't Give Up

~

"Courage doesn't always roar. Sometimes courage is the little voice at the end of the day that says I'll try again tomorrow."
~Mary Anne Radmacher

The main reason that I didn't give up on life was that I was fortunate enough to find God. Life had beaten up on me so badly. When I was fifteen, sixteen and seventeen, I found people always talking to me about how I needed to get in church and do the right thing. These were potential friends on assignment. (I'll help you to identify real friends later in this book) It was as though God was sending me messages through them. All kinds of weird things happened one after the other to pull me on track.

I mentioned that my mother was constantly on me about going to church. She realized that I was disconnected spiritually and that I needed help far beyond what any man or woman could give me. I know now that it is really hard on a woman to figure out exactly how a male child feels and exactly what to do when raising a son alone. I must credit my mom with doing her best.

My grandmother, Jessica Lester, did her part to keep me in church as a small child. She belonged to a big church downtown called Wheat Street. As long as she could, she carried me with her every Sunday. The music was good, and they had a good preacher with a big voice who told a lot of jokes. My grandmother scheduled me to be baptized. She did not know that by now I was in middle school and part of a gang. There was something about being in a gang and getting baptized that didn't seem to go together, so I decided to try and get out of the gang. I was scared to ask to get out, because I knew they might decide to kill me – that was the only way you could get out. I could not sleep for nearly a week, because it seemed that I could hear God's voice telling me to get out. I was already breaking into houses and stealing all sorts of stuff with the gang. I knew that God was sending me a warning. I also felt that asking to get out was going to cause a lot of trouble for me. I knew too much. I had seen a lot. I had too much information that could have been used against the remaining members. How did I get in such a mess? There is an old saying which says, "Trouble is easy to get into and hard to get out of." That is exactly where I found myself — in big trouble.

I finally went to the gang leaders and told them that I had to get out because I was getting baptized. I had prayed to God all night because I was so scared. When I told them what was happening, they let me go. I was so scared that I told them that after it was all over (the baptism) that I would be back. But I never went back to them. They remembered my promise and paid me back for breaking my vow. I walked into a bathroom at school and there were sixteen boys waiting for me. They turned out the light and beat me until I was bloody and bruised. One day, they even tried to kill me, but they were unsuccessful. God was protecting me.

My grandmother was bragging to her friends that I was going to be somebody special, a preacher or great speaker or something. All I knew was I had gotten the "beat down" just trying to do the right thing. Once, I was in a restaurant with some friends. We had enjoyed a good meal and then decided that we would just get up, not pay for our food and walk out. (Note: Remember when you walk out of a place like that, someone still has to pay for the meal. The money might come out of the check of a single mom who is working long hours as a waitress or server to feed her kids.) Anyway, an old lady saw what we were up to and began to talk to me as though she knew me. She told me that she knew that my great-grandmother had just died. How did she know that? Then she went on to tell me a lot of things about myself.

Then there was the night I was at a strip club with some of my friends. The club's owner was the dad of one of my friends, so we were able to get in without being twenty-one. We had no business in a place like that, but we thought it was pretty cool that we could get in because we had "connections."

One night, this guy walked up to me at the club from out of nowhere. He began to talk to me about being in a place where I did not belong. Just like with the old lady, I had never seen him before. He told me that I needed to change, and that I was born to be a leader and not a follower. He told me that I was going to have the chance to change a lot of young lives. This was so crazy because it was three o'clock in the morning and I was listening to some stranger preach to me about being a good guy. It was crazy, and it was scary. This kind of thing kept happening to me. It did not make a difference where I went or the type of people I was around or the type of places that I visited. They kept coming. The message was always the same. God was on my track like a tracking device. I knew that I had to make a quick change.

I went to a church and gave my life to Christ. I started all over again. This time my grandmother was not making arrangements for me to be baptized. I had started to make a life-changing decision for myself. I stayed at this church for a while and finally joined another ministry.

I ended up going to a place called Word of Faith in metropolitan Atlanta. I met a man whose name is Bishop Dale Bronner. He was a young, dynamic preacher who seemed to be able to look into my very soul. He had a special fire and sincerity about him that held my attention. And, even though he had not lived the rough life that I had lived, he had a lot of insight as to how things happen to a young man and the traps out there for people like me. He had "peeped my hole card." He walked tall in a gift described as "prophetic" (the ability to hear from God and interpret His Word). He was approachable. He had five children of his own. Even though he led one of the most successful ministries in the area, he found the time to make time for me. He and I communicated through emails. He respected my feelings and gave me the best advice, even if it was the complete opposite of what I might have been doing at the time. I respected him enough to take this advice and make changes as he suggested. Just like my grandmother, the old lady in the restaurant and the man outside the strip joint, Bishop Bronner saw good in me. I guess that's what the words to "Amazing Grace" mean: "I once was blind, but now I see." Looking back on it, I know that God used many people to draw me to Him. I was a "wretch" that needed special care before I fully surrendered to God. It was at Word of Faith that things really began to take shape in my life, for good. Bishop Bronner calls me "The Comeback Kid." I am grateful to have the opportunity to come back. It does not happen for everybody. Some people die in the midst of trouble and never make it back.

I went from all the painful things of my past to a life full of joy, happiness and fulfillment. I no longer had to look for girls to make me feel complete. I did not need drugs. I no longer found joy in bad behavior or the need to disrespect anyone. I found many reasons to live and began to walk with purpose. I did not want anyone to feel as I had felt. I knew that my former friends and associates were going down the wrong path. I knew they were on a fast jet to an early grave. By now, unfortunately, several of them were no longer alive. I was so filled with the love of Jesus Christ and the freedom that comes through serving Him that I knew that I had to reach back and help other young folk like myself. To do otherwise would have been like standing on the deck of a ship and watching people struggling in the water needing help. I could not let that happen. Do you remember the movie *Titanic*? According to real-life accounts of some of the actual survivors, there were many people who were willing to help those in the water while others selfishly watched people drown. In the movie version, they snatched life vests and pushed their way into lifeboats without a thought. Some of these people were supposedly best friends before the disaster.

It **MATTERS** a great deal to me that you might be reading this book, yet wanting to kill yourself at the same time. It **MATTERS** to me that you might be hooked on drugs, each time telling yourself that this will be the last time. But something always happens, and you are drawn back to "the pipe", smoking pot, or to pushing a needle into your veins. It **MATTERS** to me that you might be so caught up that you are putting your life in danger by stealing to support a habit. It **MATTERS** to me that you might be using girls (and their bodies) to help to mask the fact that you are hurting. It **MATTERS** to me that someone may be abusing you sexually (even someone in your family), and, for one reason or another, you are afraid to tell. It **MATTERS** to me that you might be a young man or young woman who is yelling and screaming with your mother or both parents on a regular basis. It **MATTERS** to me that at night when no one can hear, you may be crying yourself to sleep. It **MATTERS** to me that as you cry you might be sleeping in your car or anywhere that someone will allow you to spend the night. But, most importantly, **IT MATTERS TO GOD.**

There is a God that loves you dearly and wants to embrace you. I believe that God uses all our mistakes, flaws and even our good to shape and mold us into the people we are to become. God looks for great men and women that he can use. Before they are recognized as great, they often make a lot of mistakes. One of the runners in the 2008 Presidential campaign is a good example.

Presidential candidate Barack Obama shocked the world when he openly confessed that he had been a user of marijuana. It wasn't something that he was proud of, but something that he knew that he needed to acknowledge before "the world" and the press got a hold of it and used it against him. He beat them to the punch by publishing the whole matter in a book about his life. He took away the ammunition that they would have used against him. He did not allow the fact that he once used drugs to cripple his entire future. Like a real man, he confessed it and moved on. Today, he has been declared brilliant, powerful, and one of the greatest men in our country. He has blown the minds of people watching his progress and success at raising millions and millions of dollars from people who both listen to him and believe in him. Just suppose that he had allowed the fact that he had done something wrong to shackle his mind for the rest of his life. Just suppose that he had decided to give up.

There is this man in the Bible named Paul. He was what some would describe as a "real trip." He was a biblical "gangsta" long before me and my boys (or you and your boys) hit the street. He hated Christians, beat up on them and killed them, just because he did not like them. Well, guess what? God ended up getting a hold of Paul while he was moving on down a road to a place called Damascus, and turned him into one of His greatest preachers. He ended up traveling all around, telling others about the goodness of God and encouraging others to follow Christ. When Paul made a change, he went a full 360 degrees mentally. He started all over and came out a brand new man. People who study the Bible call Paul the greatest preacher during his time.

There is a book in the Bible that Paul wrote called Philippians. In the first chapter he wrote, "But I want you to know, Brethren, that the things which have happened to me have actually turned out for the furtherance of the gospel." When Paul wrote this, he had been through a lot. He had been shipwrecked, bitten by snakes, beaten, put in prison and involved in many other troubles. He came out of all of it determined to do what he was called to do. In other words, he made a big change.

There are some things that will come into our lives and pull us back, set us back, hold us back, and even take us back. Whether these things are wrong relationships, bad decisions, or careless thinking, they all have a tendency to cause an uncomfortable feeling within. These same experiences can end up being the driving force that propels us forward. It's like using a slingshot.

The slingshot is a "Y"-shaped stick with an elastic band attached for shooting small stones. In order to shoot the small stones, you have to pull a rubber band stretched between the two forks of the stick. The further back you pull the band with the stone, the further it will go when you release it. In other words, you might have sunk really low and become involved in some pretty bad stuff. That same "trouble" might be the stone for your slingshot. Your stone may take you a long way into the future. Look at me. I could not encourage you like this if I had not messed up so badly. Even though I tried to prove that I could live like a devil, everything that I did became textbook material for me to help you.

If I had given up, I would have let so many people down. Firstly, I would have disappointed God. Secondly, I would have added to my mother's pain. I would have denied her the right and pleasure of having a good son. I would have denied her the right to feel she is a good mother. Thirdly, I would have cheated myself by ruining any chance to become the person that God has called me to be. I don't care what you have done in life – there is still hope. If no one else has the faith that you can turn it around, then I will be the person who dares to see hope for your future. All you need is one person to stand in agreement with you and, in the words of the once-popular song, "Here I am, baby."

God's word says that if you and I agree, according to God's will, then it will be done.

"Again, I say to you, whatsoever you bind on earth will be bound in heaven, and whatsoever you loose on earth will be loosed in heaven." Matthew 18:19

Even though the Bible was written a long time ago, and you might not understand it, there are a lot of promises in there that are about you, what you are going through and the plans that God has for your life —yes, you.

Today, I reach out to those of you who are in great pain, not from sickness or from physical injury, but from wounds of loneliness, deception, disappointment, and all the other things that have brought you to this point. I believe that we are all stones on the rubber band of God's slingshot. I believe God is preparing us to be propelled into our destiny. Therefore, I proclaim that your suffering is not in vain, but for glory and honor that no earthly man can steal. In other words, we are prepared by pain and propelled by God. This is why I just could not give up. This is why you can't, either. You cannot afford it. Remember the words in Matthew 18:19.

Please read this prayer with me. It represents the fact that I stand with you in agreement. The Word says that a marvelous and heavenly partnership happens when we come together and believe. The Bible says that if you pray alone, you have power, but if we pray together then that power is increased to ten times as much. It states, "one can chase a thousand, two can chase ten thousand" Deuteronomy 32:30.

I'd like for you to repeat these words of prayer and meditation if you are at a place in your life where you want to change in a certain area, but you feel that nothing is working. There are times that we are able to make the correction inside, but then there are other times where God Himself has to perfect [fix] the change within that needs to take place. I don't want you to feel as if this is something you have to do, but in the Bible, when the great King David got discouraged (look at I Samuel 30:6), and the crowd wanted to stone him, he needed encouragement. There was no one else there to do it, so he encouraged himself.

There are times where you will feel totally alone, and the only person who will be able to encourage you will be you — and, of course, God. Please repeat these words and say them to God. I am in agreement with you that you will change.

PRAYER

Lord,

Sometimes I just want to give up. My burdens are overwhelming. I don't seem ever to catch up. I can't seem to get started. I feel the pain of stress, hurt, and delay. I have done things that I know I need to change, but I have a hard time making my change permanent.

There are also a lot of things that I have going on in my life that I just don't understand. I ask you to help me to change for good so that I may live a long and healthy life.

Please strengthen me to stand up, knowing you are always with me. Help me know that it is not what people call me, but what I answer to. Please help me to know that it is not how I start, but how I finish, and that I finish as a winner.

Help me to run the race of life with wisdom and patience. Restore the broken places in my life so that I won't hurt in them, and then I may use those healed wounds to help someone else.

I decree today that I will change and never look back, that I will be more than average, that I will do great things while I'm granted life, that I'll be a blessing even to those who have done me wrong. I will have peace and trust in you. I want to have the resources and love required to provide for me and eventually for my family. I desire the energy and motivation to perform my job, work, and daily tasks at home, school, or wherever I am in life.

Please give me a fresh breeze of release to lighten my load. Send the right people in my life to be a source of love, guidance, and new opportunities. God, give me faith in myself, not only on the days when I am doing great and winning and nothing seems impossible, but on days when I wonder if I am brave enough, smart enough, or strong enough. Please don't let me quit — not ever, God.

Please help me to keep faith in myself no matter how many people discourage me, doubt me, laugh at me, warn me, think of me as a fool, or refuse to listen to me. Let me hear another voice telling me, "You can do it, and you will."

If no one else in the world seems to care or believe in me, please help me to believe in myself. I know there will be times when I will doubt my own ability; I might become discouraged, or find myself on the verge of despair. Please don't let me give up. Please hang on to me.

Fan the fires of my faith so that I will try even harder. Give me even more faith in myself. You are the source of my strength, abilities, and my faith. I know that you will give me what I ask for: faith in myself through your power and glory.

Thank You, Lord, for hearing me out. I am ready for the serenity, peace and solutions you adapt to the changes in my life.

Amen

Keep this prayer with you. I hope it blesses your life. Anytime you feel as though you need to release your cares to someone, say a prayer or write down your innermost thoughts.

Chapter 6

Love Letters

~

"Where there is love, there is life."

~Mahatma Gandhi

Love letters usually begin early in childhood. As soon as little children learn to read, write, and form sentences, they often begin to write little things to each other like, "Roses are Red, Violets are Blue, Sugar is Sweet, and So are You." Later in life (during the teen years) we try to find better ways to write love letters. We begin to look for different and more meaningful words that express our feelings. Some of the most powerful love letters that you can receive will come from people who love you because they care about you as a person. They are not thinking about themselves.

This is one of the letters that I received from my mom when I was still acting out my pain. She showed love even when I was taking her car, messing up her house, and showing her a lot of disrespect. A praying mother has a lot of power over your life.

From My Mom…

Dear Terence,

Hi! Hope you're doing just fine. I am very proud of you for striving to earn a degree.

I am disappointed that you chose to act very disrespectfully last week. You drove my car while I was out of town, you argued back with me on the telephone without showing respect, you argued with your dad, and you left dirty dishes in my house.

To you, all of that may seem very small; however, as you mature as an adult those are big issues. First of all, your spirit of disrespect and using ugly language when things don't go your way in no way shows maturity. As an adult, you will not

41

have your way all the time. You need to deal with your ANGER problem. This is very serious. The problem will hold you back from having a decent job and a good relationship with a nice young lady. I tell you these things because I love you and I want the BEST for you. If I allow you to disrespect me, you will never change to the outside world. Also, please be clean and neat in your home. It is important, and it's a reflection of you.

Terence, I LOVE you, but you need to hear the truth! I pray for you every day that one day you'll be successful.

The real test for you, as an adult, will be when you graduate from a four-year college, become a teacher, land a job, and pay your own bills.

One thing you must remember as well is not to allow a female to trap you with a baby right now. Wait until you have finished college and have established your life. Having a child at the wrong time would be a setback for your future and the things you have said that you want to do. I just thought I needed to mention that while I have your attention, because I want you to be the person you want to be one day.

I am praying to God to REMOVE the spirit of ANGER and DISRESPECT from you. Terence, you are a goodhearted person. I know that you can change the ANGER. If you need help, I will be there for you.

Mom

Eventually, I got my act together and found a wonderful woman to be my wife. Remember, one of the things that my Mom wanted for me was to have a decent person to walk beside me. She did not want me to be "trapped" because I had gotten someone pregnant. That almost happened to me in an earlier relationship; however, the pregnancy ended after the young woman had problems with her health.

It was after I changed my life that I found the sweetest and most precious woman that a man could ever want. She wasn't the type of girl that I had known before. She was different. She writes me notes of encouragement from time to time, such as the one below. A lot went on in my life between my mom's letter and my wife's. I thank God for everything that took place between the times that they wrote me.

From My Wife…………

Babe,

I love you so much! You are a blessing to me. I am so glad God gave you to me as a husband. You are a great man. And I know you will be a great father to our children and a great counselor to the nation. It is well! We are going to do mighty things for the Kingdom. We are a great team. I love laughing with you, because I like to see you happy.

Love Always,
Cee-Cee

DECISIONS THAT MAKE YOU OR BREAK YOU

Chapter 7

Can You Find Yourself Here?

~

"Finding common ground never hurt anyone."

~Terence B. Lester

Meaningful Moments with Young People

Recently, while holding a conversation with about twenty-five young people, I asked how many of them felt that entertainment could educate them. Much to my surprise about twenty of them raised their hands to indicate that they felt that they could receive an education through pure entertainment. I felt the need to explain that entertainment is just that. It makes you feel good for a while, but its value is much less than an education that lasts a lifetime.

I am not against entertainment, but I am against anything that takes the place of education. I am against the way entertainment holds more weight in the lives of young people than gaining knowledge that will carry them through many situations requiring thought and intelligence.

Over and over, I hear the very same stories pouring out of young people. These are some comments from young people in a public school. Sometimes I wonder if we enter school buildings with so much anger and baggage of frustration that school and family just seem to be aggravations rather than a part of the plan to move us forward. I believe in "keeping the main thing the main thing." I feel that we should seek knowledge and not expect the world always to give us a beat or stand on its head to get our attention. Can you find yourself in any of these testimonies?

****

"One thing that bothers me at school is that the teachers always blame things on me, because I have a reputation. I do a lot of bad things, make bad decisions, but because of my reputation I get blamed for a lot of things that I really did not do."

47

****

"Sometimes I come to school and don't want to be bothered, but some teacher is always going to say something which is going to make me mad."

****

"What's getting on my nerves in the last few weeks is family and school. My family is getting on my nerves, because they are dumb and stupid. I don't talk to them. They are all selfish, and I just don't like them. School is getting on my nerves, because the teachers think they can do anything. They talk to us like they own us. They say we can't wear flip-flops. What do flip-flops have to do with school, anyway?"

****

"I feel I have no one to talk to, and that hurts me. I feel alone, so sometimes I just keep to myself, but that's hard. But one thing that cheers me up is my Grandma. But she's gone now. My teachers get on my nerves because some of them don't want to teach you, but only want to make your life worse. One of my teachers doesn't even teach. She just stays on her laptop. Then she gets mad when we finish our work and start talking because we have nothing else to do."

****

"What's messing with me is when I get in trouble for no reason. People want to fight me for no reason. People get smart with me, and I get smart back. But when I get smart, they get an attitude. Then there is my mother. She tells everyone about me. She tells them what I am doing, what I am saying, and everything else. My dad doesn't believe me about anything."

****

"School is supposed to make you smarter, give you some education, but that is not the case. School is like a war zone. There are fights all the time. Learning is supposed to be fun, so why do we sit around reading books in class and have test after test? Why can't we learn, but have fun learning? I can't understand why, when one person does something wrong, the whole class goes down with them. Teachers don't have time to listen to the students, so a lot of students have to take actions for themselves — fighting and cursing."

****

In life we will all have problems. We all fall down at times, but how we are falling is the problem. An entire generation is falling to drugs, guns, idols, clothes, cars, violence, sex, and, most of all, bad attitudes. This generation is being raised by products and marketing, schemes, fads, trends, ideologies, and images. What they really need are parents, real love, respect, and discipline. The world is becoming so creative that we have forgotten who created it. What has more influence in your life right now, your clothes and your friends, or getting an education and making something of yourself? Is God getting any of your time or any attention from you? Are you forgetting the meaning of school and God's plan for you to be successful?

Many of these students in the comments above had what I would call a "Victim Complex." They always felt as though the world was out to get them. They brought to the table a lot of pain. Most of the time, they did not own up to the fact that their reaction to the pain and their attitude posed a real problem and that this negative attitude got to the school building long before they reached it. Perhaps some of them had valid concerns, but they handled them wrongly, and their attitude placed them in a position where people did not want to hear what they had to say.

I can say all of this because I have been there. I am still young enough that I can "feel" where you are in life. Often this victim complex has pain as its root source.

49

Let me share a piece that I wrote. It is called *"Seeing Past the Pain."*

When there's a pain, there's a healing,
When there's sorrow, there's a joy,
When there's pressure, there's a breakthrough,
When there's rain, there's an umbrella,
Where there's heat, something's getting ready,
When things are slow, preparation is taking place,
Where there's mediocrity, there's wealth,
Where there's discouragement, there's courage,
Where there's discomfort, there's growth,
Where there's confusion, there's time to reveal,
When it seems like an untouchable goal, remember there's an
untouchable God,
Where there's hunger, there's a multitude,
When there's lack, there's relief,
When tears fall, there's a heart being cleansed,
When there's hurt, there's poetry,
When there's opposition, there's triumph,
Where there's fear, there's fire,
Where there's a roadblock, there's a detour.

We have to see past the pain, and past the tears.

--Terence B. Lester

Chapter 8

Who Floats Your Boat?
(Relationships)

~

"If you let the wrong people sail your boat for you, they'll sink it."
~Terence B. Lester

Now let's look at the kinds of things that can absolutely wreck your life. Life is definitely a journey. It's almost like a long voyage on the ocean. You may encounter storms on the trip. There may be high winds and tough waves. The question is, "Who is in charge of your boat? Exactly whom are you allowing to serve as your navigator?"

Being in a relationship is like a test, a test of how you treat yourself and how you treat others. Friendships and relationships require that all parties work on the "friendship" so that it will not fail. You must first cherish yourself and develop relationships with positive action. People who don't love themselves do a really good job of linking up with the wrong folk. There is an old song whose lyrics share a powerful message that "no man is an island and no man stands alone." This is how we end up needing others to walk this path, called "life," with us.

Friends are important for a bunch of different reasons. Firstly, they support each other emotionally (they've got your back). Secondly, they remain with you through good times and bad. Thirdly, they are willing to see things from the other's point of view and will provide help and constructive criticism when needed. Fourthly, they help each other enjoy new experiences and appreciate life more fully.

I have several great friendships that mean an awful lot to me. While each friendship is unique, there are some shared ideas and expectations about what friendship means. Everyone you call your friend might not actually be whom you need in your life. Why not put your friendships to a test? Here are some qualities of a good friendship. Ask yourself some questions about each friendship that you have.

Just look at the people whom you spend a lot of time with and call friends. Ask yourself if these relationships bring any **comfort.** Or do you find yourself trying to measure up and explain yourself all of the time? Are these people **willing to listen** to you, rather than tell you what to do? Do these individuals **accept** you the way you are, or do they spend a lot of time trying to make you somebody that you don't want to be? Do you feel like they **appreciate** you, or do you feel like you are the "Good Ole Joe" that has to make them happy? Do these individuals "have your back?" Do you ever receive **encouragement,** or do you find yourself providing encouragement, but receiving little in exchange?

If your friends lead you down the wrong path, beat you down with criticism, or are not "there for you" when things get tough, then maybe you don't have a friendship. Maybe it is just an acquaintance or associate relationship, rather than a friendship. Remember that a good friendship will at some point provide the following:

- Comfort
- Someone to talk to who will listen and try to understand
- Reasonable acceptance
- Appreciation of you as a human being
- Encouragement

When I found myself in trouble, many times my "boys" ran out on me and left me to face the consequences alone. If I had money, I had friends. If I were broke, I didn't have as many. Were they really my friends? If they gave me drugs, were they my friends or my enemies? If they helped me to steal cars and joyride, were they actually trying to help me?

Sometimes there were people around me who reminded me that I knew better and that the things I did were wrong. They tried their best to keep me out of trouble. They thought enough of me to try to get me to accept the possibility that I might get in trouble. They did it because they cared for me. These were my true friends, and I didn't know it.

Recently, there was a message floating around on the Internet about people and the purpose they play in our lives. Like most chain emails, it does not give a name of an author. I don't always pay these emails any attention, but this one actually gave me a lot to think about:

"People come into your life for a reason, a season or a lifetime. When you know which one it is, you will know what to do for that person. When someone is in your life for a REASON, it is usually to meet a need you have expressed. They have come to assist you through a difficulty, to provide you with guidance and support, to aid you physically, emotionally or spiritually. They may seem like a Godsend, and sometimes they are. They are there for the reason you need them to be. Then, without any wrongdoing on your part or at an inconvenient time, this person will say or do something to bring the relationship to an end.

Sometimes they die. Sometimes they walk away. Sometimes they act up and force you to take a stand. What we must realize is that our need has been met, our desire fulfilled, their work is done. The prayer you sent up has been answered, and now it is time to move on.

Some people come into your life for a SEASON, because your turn has come to share, grow or learn. They bring you an experience of peace or make you laugh. They may teach you something you have never done. They usually give you an unbelievable amount of joy. Believe it, it is real. But it comes only for a season.

Your job is to accept the lesson, love the person, and put what you have learned to use in all other relationships and areas of your life. It is said that love is blind, but friendship is clairvoyant."

You probably have friends that "had your back" in a couple of situations. They might have "been there" for you when you needed a couple of dollars, didn't have a ride, or had no one else to listen

53

to you. At the time, they performed in the capacity of a friend. However, what you owe these individuals is gratitude, not your entire life. Are they going in a direction that won't help you to achieve your goals?

Les Brown, a famous motivational speaker, states that if you look at your five closest friends, you will see that your life will be very similar to theirs. He has even done studies on adults and their associates. According to him, most individuals that are close associates tend to make the same amount of money and do similar things. If you are hanging with a gang banger on the corner, even though he is a "Good Ole Joe," guess what? You might be headed for the same dangerous lifestyle. Maybe you have been friends since you were little kids, but let me ask this question, "Are you willing to follow this person to an early death?" Would you like to be dressed up in a fine suit, decked out in "bling," and lying next to them in a box in a lush, green cemetery? That makes it a little different, doesn't it? I certainly hope so.

I am reminded of the powerful influence of both Tupac Shakuar and Biggie Smalls. They had the power to lead individuals in any direction that they chose. People went out of their way to be seen with them and to be known as their friends, but both were shot down in public. Tupac was shot down on the streets in Las Vegas, and Biggie Smalls died on the streets of Los Angeles. A lot of people saw what happened. Guess what? Everybody who saw both incidents has chosen to remain silent for obvious reasons. When the bullets started to fly, friendships with both of them went to another dynamic. The picture changed altogether. The people around them weren't thinking about telling what they knew. It's called self-preservation. They have the right to protect themselves in this situation. You also have a right to preserve your life by weighing every relationship and every motive. Ask yourself the following questions:

- What does this person want from me?

- How can this person fit into my life's plan?

- How can the two of us be a positive blessing to each other?

- Is it possible that being with this person will not be good for me?

- Will I eventually get into trouble because of association with this person?

If you are unsure about some or all of these questions, then maybe you need some new friendships.

Chapter 9

Check Your Actions

~

"Actions determine what we get in life."
~*Terence B. Lester*

"Action is the antidote to despair."
~*Joan Baez*

I wrote this story for a homeless man that I met one Christmas:

It was a very cold Christmas Eve. The stores were really packed, and people were shopping for Christmas gifts. Everybody was buying and spending, but no one was really focused on the true meaning of the word "present." That day, while everyone was shopping for each other and themselves, it just so happened that there was a homeless man standing outside a store filled with shoppers.

As he stood there in the cold with nothing to eat, no warm clothes or any support, he asked and begged people for a couple of dollars to get something to eat. There was no response. Everyone walked pass him like he wasn't even there. Some people even told him to get a job. The man continued to beg and beg, but still there was no answer.

Now considering that is a time for giving, it seemed like everybody was only focused on shopping for presents. All of a sudden, a young man walked up to the old man and said, "Listen, sir, I don't have much myself, but here is two of the five dollars I have."

The old man smiled. He looked at the young man and asked, "How old are you?"

The young man replied, "Twenty-one, sir."

The old man paused for a moment and then asked, "Why do you give this to a homeless man?"

The young man looked into his eyes and replied, "I also know what it feels like to be homeless. I have a family that I live with, but since the communication is negative, all the warm feelings of home have been taken away. Without true communication or a solid relationship, I feel homeless, just like you. Without love, there isn't a home. People walk around ignoring the fact that everyone isn't as fortunate as they are to have a family. People should be grateful of "presence" and not grateful only to buy presents. You can't buy real presence. No matter what they think of you and how you are being ignored, I understand."

All of a sudden, the man said, "Follow me." He led the young man into the store all the way to the back. To the young man's surprise, the homeless man owned the store and was very wealthy. He told the young man that he had approached shoppers in his store for the last ten years just to see if anyone would show any real compassion. He reminded him that even though his store was in one the richest neighborhoods in the city, no one had given a dime to the homeless.

The old man said to the young man, "I'm your new home; I'm going to be your friend."

Some people need to realize that shopping eventually wears out, but real "presence" will always be with you. The moral of the story is that you'll never know how you will help yourself by your actions in helping and being a present help to someone else. The "presents" you buy wear out, but the "presence" you give leaves a mark in the hearts of many.

If you truly have a strong passion for what you want, a desire to pursue that goal persistently, and a personal commitment to take action, you can achieve almost anything, no matter how large or unattainable a goal may appear. Lao Tzu stated it well: "A journey of a thousand miles begins with one step."

Successful people plan and implement continual action towards their goals. Even when those actions produce a negative result, they provide experience to modify other actions and attain a result that is closer to that ultimate goal. When it comes to action, I believe that the head and the heart play a big role in the outcome. Allow me to make some comparisons with the head and the heart and show you exactly what I mean.

Here are twelve things that can tell us if a person is using their head or their heart:

1. The head will cause a person to have a negative attitude. The heart causes a person to have an optimistic outlook.

2. The head will cause a person to become angry easily. The heart causes a person to make peace over and over again.

3. The head causes a person to assume. The heart causes a person to research.

4. The head causes a person to gossip. The heart will cause a person to stay away from gossip.

5. The head says, "Me…me…me." The heart says, "Them…them…them."

6. The head speaks discouragement. The heart speaks encouragement.

7. The head reacts, then thinks. The heart thinks, then acts.

8. The head compromises to get ahead in life. The heart stays true, even if it means staying behind.

9. The head says, "I don't care." The heart says, "How can I help?"

10. The head says, "I know it all," and becomes stubborn. The heart asks, "Can you teach me?" and becomes teachable.

11. The head is filled with pride and will hold grudges. The heart is filled with love and will spread joy.

12. The head wants to portray someone else and forget about his or her original identity. The heart seeks the image of God.

There is a big difference between the head and the heart, and many times, we get them confused. You'll know if it is the heart speaking, because it never has to think about truth. I believe that if we cleanse our hearts and do things out of love, a lot of our problems will be eliminated. I believe that we should focus on our actions a lot more and try to improve them daily. When we focus on others, it throws our focus off. Let me explain. I'm reminded of a story that I wrote about two fishermen:

One day, there were two guys fishing. One was dressed in a raincoat and the other was dressed in shorts and flip-flops. The guy in the flip-flops leaned over to the guy wearing the raincoat and said, "There sure is a lot of sun out," with a sarcastic tone and laughed aloud. The man in the raincoat remained silent and said nothing. Hours after fishing, it began to rain vigorously. The guy with the shorts and the flip-flops got drenched. Afterwards, the guy with the raincoat said these words to the guy wearing the shorts and flip-flops, "I prepared yesterday for today's storm."

The moral of the story is that if you do what needs to be done today, then tomorrow's rain will not affect you as much. If we act the way we are supposed to act, we won't have time to focus on someone else. We must understand that whatever or whoever angers us, controls us.

How I Act Determines What I Attract

We have to watch our actions very closely, because we don't attract what we want in life; we attract who we are. For example, I know a young man that is always getting himself into bad situations. He has been arrested, gotten into plenty of fights, and doesn't feel that good about himself. Let me try to explain. It's actually very simple.

All of his actions have attracted everything that has happened to him. If you run a red light in front of a police officer, you can't expect your actions not to attract the police officer and a ticket. If you are in the kitchen cooking over a hot stove and you decide to touch the hot stove with your bare hands, you can expect to get burned. I want you to know that whatever you do results in a consequence or a reward.

60

If you want to attract the good things in life, you must change your actions. If you want to become a successful business owner, you will not accomplish this goal by sleeping every day. If you want to become a doctor, a lawyer, or an athlete, all of these professions require a plan and the right actions in life (Positive Practice). In summary, as Dale Bronner says, "We don't receive what we want in life; we receive what we prepare for and act upon."

Habits and how they can control your outcome

First, allow me to explain what a habit happens to be. A habit is a pattern of behavior that's repeated. People are often not aware of their habits. It has been said, "First, you form a habit, and then the habit forms you." This is true in so many ways, because what we do on a daily basis is what we can expect to continue to do. Let me give you some examples of good and bad habits and how they affect us:

Good Habits

1. **Reading** – This is a good habit because it can increase your knowledge and wisdom. Almost all leaders are readers.

2. **Writing poetry or music** – This gives you a chance to open yourself up and release a lot of things that you might otherwise internalize. This habit can be used to channel anger. It has helped me tremendously.

3. **Playing a sport or games** – These types of activities can redirect anger and even produce peace and relief by taking your mind off something negative and focusing it on something positive. It is also good in maintaining a healthy body, mind and soul. Remember, whatever you focus on, you move towards. Try to have fun.

4. **Being polite** - Good manners will take you further than degrees, preparation, networking, or ability.

5. **Going to church** - Churches and church people may not be perfect, but Christians serve the perfect God. There are many people who acknowledge that a relationship with God helps them to become better people. Make it a habit to go to church and meet other young people whose goals are positive. It is a good place to start.

6. **Seeing a world of other possibilities** – I might not have said everything, but there are tons of things out there, like joining clubs, walking, riding a bike, traveling, and shopping. Whatever helps you mentally can turn a negative mindset into a positive mindset.

Bad Habits

1. **Smoking** – It promotes bad health and potentially shortens your life.

2. **Cursing** – It builds a wall around true self-expression. It indicates an inadequate vocabulary. It becomes an addiction to a frustrated mind. As soon as the frustrated mind becomes upset, it will rattle off and curse before expressing itself in a more appropriate manner. It shows a level of ignorance that is totally unnecessary.

3. **Lying** – Never let lying become a habit, because it begins to hide you from yourself.

4. **Cheating** – Never be so caught up in winning that you cheat yourself or others. I remember cheating on a lot of tests in school that I knew I could have done on my own. Cheating also produces physical and mental laziness.

5. **Bad manners and disrespect** – If you want your reputation to be bad and guarantee that doors of opportunity will slam in your face, then just be rude, act ugly, and devalue other human beings.

These are some of the habits that many people have today. Habits develop subconsciously through what you do on a daily basis, such as the entertainment you choose, what you watch on television, what you surround yourself with, and what you listen to. The next time you feel yourself picking up any type of bad habit rather than a good habit, stop in your tracks before it becomes a problem. Remember, feed yourself things that will help you in building your character, and surround yourself with positive individuals who have traveled the path you are seeking.

Lights, Camera, Action

Practically everyone wants to be known, loved, and shown that they are appreciated, but do not let that become your goal. I remember in high school, some of my goals were to be known in the lights, be shown on the camera, and have the coolest actions. In other words, I wanted to fit in and be accepted so badly, I did everything I could to make it happen. It became one of my main priorities. I'm here to tell you that trying to fit in with the crowd is not the way to go. Why? It robs your focus from developing yourself. Trust me, if I were still hanging around the "in" crowd, you would not be reading this book today. If you want to be known, become a positive leader for others to follow.

Chapter 10

How Far Will Your Attitude Take You?

~

"A positive attitude is a person's passport to a better tomorrow."
~Unknown

"Attitude is an attraction in your theme park."
~Terence B. Lester

I can remember my mother, my father, and both of my grandmothers, as well as a lot of other people talking to me about how important it is to have a good attitude. People will look at you not only for who you are, but also for how you handle life. An unpleasant attitude is just like wearing a sign that says, "Count me out. Don't give me any breaks. Treat me as though you don't want to be bothered. Ignore me, and look for someone else."

People are drawn to positive and receptive people. An angry or unappreciative attitude will cause people to hold back the good that they would otherwise do for you. They will also have less respect for what you have to say and will not give you the attention that they would make available to someone who presented themselves differently.

Attitude is the single most important trait. It makes or breaks us. In fact, regardless of our profession, position, background, or talent, our attitude can either help every single, solitary aspect of behavior and decision-making, or destroy every single thing we touch. A negative attitude can stunt our growth tremendously. A positive attitude can lead us to success, happiness and joy, while a negative attitude can leave us doomed to failure forever.

A great thing about having a positive attitude is that it's totally under your control. Maybe we can't control everything that happens to us, but we are definitely in control of our attitude toward everything that happens to us. It is true that others may influence your attitude, but ultimately you are the master of your attitude. You are in the driver's seat.

I want you to see that we might be right in a lot of situations, but our attitude can work against us and cause us to be wrong.

Here is something I found very interesting concerning the attitude: I call it the "Victim and the Predator Syndrome."

There are a lot of times that we become victims. In some of these instances, our goals may be totally harmless, but we become a predator and take everything out on those around us. Here is what I found out about the Victim and the Predator Syndrome.

First, I thought about both words, "victim" and "predator." As I thought about them in depth, I found that there is actually a very thin line between the two. We can become victims by simply being in a position where our family, associates, friends, or even our own problems wrong us. At times, I have felt victimized by a number of people, but if I hadn't had the right attitude, it would have held me back. These are things that we can't control, but we can decide how we respond to them. I also understand that many people fall victim to hurting others because they have been hurt in the past. They feel like life has dealt them a bad hand, so they want to "scramble someone else's deck."

There is a principle by John Maxwell that says, "Hurt people, hurt people." They live the life of both the victim and the predator. The predator is one who is out to devour the prey at any cost. The predator will not be happy unless he or she has done their job of ruining another person's situation. I believe, as we all are faced with circumstances, it is not how we react, but how we respond that determines our outcome. We need to have a good attitude.

I pray that today you will begin to see past the hurts of any individual who may have mistreated you or harmed you and understand that we all are nothing without God. Our attitude is deeply connected to our well-being. Or, let's put it this way, our well-being depends upon our attitude. We must learn how to respond to whatever life throws at us. "Instead of reacting irrationally, we've got to respond righteously."

Here is a passage by Charles Swindoll on attitude that I think will help us understand it better:

"The longer I live, the more I realize the impact of attitude on life. Attitude, to me, is more important than facts. It is more important than the past, than education, than money, than circumstances, than failures, than success, than what other

people think or say or do. It is more important than appearance, giftedness or skill. It will make or break a company...a church...a home. The remarkable thing is we have a choice every day regarding the attitude we will embrace for that day. We cannot change the past...we cannot change the fact that people will act in a certain way. We cannot change the inevitable. The only thing we can do is play on the one string we have and that is our ATTITUDE...I am convinced that life is 10% what happens to you and 90% how you react to it. And so it is with you...we are in charge of our attitudes."

This is so true regarding how much our attitude affects every part of our life.

One day when I was looking in the mirror, I realized that it's not the reflection in the mirror that counts. Rather, it's the reflection from within that creates the image in the mirror. The way we feel on the inside about ourselves ultimately creates our outward image. We need to have confidence in what we see and feel in ourselves, instead of depending upon the mirror.

We create unnecessary barricades with a limited vision. Basically, the things we cannot see within ourselves are the same things we cannot visualize for ourselves. We should be mindful of how we view ourselves, because we can be our worst enemy simply by the way we view things and how we force others to look at us. We must remember that the "inner" appearance really shapes the "outer" appearance. If you are tired of hearing that your attitude needs to improve, then I would like to offer a handy list of ways to make that 360° turn mentally.

Here are ten ways to maintain a positive attitude:

1. **Appreciate yourself and your value.** Valuing yourself can prevent discipline problems, offer a natural way for you to feel good about yourself, and give you a chance to learn something new everyday. This is essential in the foundation of a positive relationship with yourself. I also had to learn that the relationship that you have with yourself affects every relationship that you have with others.

2. **Listen before responding.** It's important to make eye contact with everyone who is speaking to you. I had a real problem at first with this, but became better at it once I realized that we learn a lot if we pay attention. I believe that listening trains our patience in responding to life's problems.

3. **Build yourself up.** You must learn to encourage yourself. Do not count on your friends or peers for encouragement. If you put all of your faith in human beings, you will probably be let down eventually. Watch, listen, and work to surround yourself with individuals and opportunities that will begin to build you up.

4. **Be grateful, honest, and respectful, and have integrity.** All of these are qualities of a well-rounded individual. Today, I try my best to exhibit each of these qualities at their full potential daily. I never say that I have mastered them all, because we all make mistakes and we are not perfect. But these qualities are good goals to try to reach daily. They will help shape your attitude in a tremendous way.

5. **Know and develop your unique talents.** Talents, gifts, and abilities are all connected to our purpose for living. I believe the more I begin to focus on my gifts, the more clarity comes to me as to what I am to do in life. Remember, focus is a powerful thing. Whatever you focus on, that's the direction in which you'll end up going. If you have not identified your gifts, then find an area that you admire and experiment with opportunities until you find your purpose.

I've heard my pastor state, "Practice does not make perfect, but it surely makes you better" (Bishop Dale C. Bronner).

6. **Cherish your time.** Your time is your most valuable asset. Don't waste it, because you cannot replace it. If I didn't get myself together within a certain time frame, I'd probably be

dead. It is possible to participate in negative behavior for too long. You have to decide where you want to be and then make that decision to get there. Remember, how you spend your time is how your time will pay off in the future.

7. **Set your focus.** Find out where you want to go, and then go after it. Remember, though, if you do not know where you're going, any road will take you there.

8. **Take care of your health.** If you are tired, ill or just worn out, you cannot be effective. Eat healthy, get enough sleep, take occasional breaks from life (vacation or vent) if possible, and get the support of family, friends and neighbors when things seem overwhelming. Remember, you want to maintain your health so you can enjoy your future.

9. **Be responsible.** Responsibility trains you for your future. Do not cheat yourself of responsibility. If you do, you will cripple yourself.

10. **Never stop learning.** You should never end the search for the understanding of right and wrong. We will never reach our maximum potential unless we face reality. That's why we should develop from within and first learn about the person within as a unique individual.

I remember a story that someone shared with me while they were skimming through their e-mail. It is a forward that was circulating through e-mails by an unknown author. It gives a clear understanding on how to shape your attitude. It's called, "The Carpenter":

There was an elderly carpenter who was ready for retirement. He told his employer-contractor about his plans to leave the house-building business to live a more leisurely life with his wife and enjoy his extended family. He indicated that he would miss the paycheck each week, but he wanted to retire, and he felt he and his family would survive financially.

The contractor was sorry to see his good worker leave and asked if he could build just one more house as a personal favor. The carpenter said yes, but over time it was easy to see that his heart was not in his work. He resorted to sloppy workmanship and used inferior materials. It was an unfortunate way to end a dedicated career.

When the carpenter finished his work, his employer came to inspect the house. Then he handed the front door key to the carpenter and said, "This is your house...my gift to you."

The carpenter was shocked! What a shame! If he had only known he was building his own house, he would have done it all so differently.

We build our lives a day at a time often putting less than our best into the building. Then, with a shock, we realize we have to live in the house we have built. If we could do it over, we would do it differently and better.

But you cannot go back to the past. You are the carpenter and every day you hammer a nail, place a board or move a wall; you build a foundation. Someone once said, "Life is a do-it-yourself project." Your attitude and the choices you make today helps build the "house" you will live in tomorrow. Therefore, build wisely!

-Unknown

Sometimes our attitudes are bad because we feel misunderstood. A lot of times, misunderstanding comes from a lack of communication. I felt like nobody understood me when I was younger, because I held a lot of things inside. There were older adults around that I could have talked to, but since I felt like they wouldn't understand, I felt like no one understood me. The best way to get across that bridge is to cross it.

I believe that if you are facing problems in an area that really hurts you, you should get up enough courage and find a good person to talk to that can relate to you and advise you in that area. Please note, I said a "good" person. There are a lot of examples of the wrong people in the world that would love to talk to you. So you must be careful in selecting someone to talk to. It's not as hard as it might seem. You just have to look for the ten things that true friends communicate. According to David and Teresa Ferguson, positive relationships usually cause us to experience some or all of the following:

1. Comfort
2. Attention
3. Acceptance
4. Appreciation
5. Support
6. Encouragement
7. Affection
8. Respect
9. Security
10. Approval

Once, I listened to a speaker who made remarks that remain with me today. He said, "What I think controls who I am and ultimately affects my attitude and how others perceive me. Others will 'read' my attitude and decide if they want to be around me at all."

In summary, what you think not only controls who you are, it controls your outlook on life and how you perceive things: your focus, actions, self-esteem, confidence, influence, emotions, happiness, anger, habits, and the dreams you want to achieve. The list goes on and on. We must understand that "life is the only canvas where we can paint our outcome with what we think." It was Henry Ford who observed, "Whether you think that you can, or that you can't, you are usually right." Our thinking plays a very important role in becoming the great person who we were created to be.

In many instances, the crowd can't help you. In fact, they may be a part of your having an unpleasant attitude. As you can see from my experiences, the crowd can lead you astray. I heard a wise man once say, "If you run with the crowd, you'll get no farther than the crowd." And that, "Birds of a feather not only flock together, they also fly to the same destination." I am a living witness, and probably many others will confess that the crowd is not the best choice.

Trust me, I know what you're thinking: "It's hard." Sure, it might be hard to leave the crowd, but look at it this way, the crowd can stop you from ever becoming more than average.

I suspect that you don't want to live just an average life, but doing the same things without adjustment will never result in real progress in life. I believe that if you ever began to make a decision to have a great attitude, then you will become a leader and set positive examples. Then the crowd will follow you. You can make a difference and have a major impact on the lives of other individuals while having a positive attitude.

Chapter 11

"Gossip": The Silent Killer

~

"Whoever gossips to you will gossip about you!"
~Spanish Proverb

"Gossip is hearing something you like about someone you don't."
~Earl Wilson

"Silent gossiping can destroy a loud crowd."
~Terence B. Lester

Are you a Murderer?

Gossip has the capacity literally to kill a person. Sometimes we participate in conversations that are not based on facts. Many times people are speculating or making guesses. This can really hurt people.

Over the years, I've found that the one thing that will literally destroy any relationship, partnership, or any kind of friendship is gossip. Gossip is a powerful weapon and silent killer. We must understand that words have great power, and the way we use them may impact us either positively or negatively. That's why I believe we should think before we speak. I would like to share with you a poem by an unknown author explaining exactly what gossip is. It's entitled, "My Name is Gossip."

My Name is Gossip

My name is Gossip.
I have no respect for justice.
I maim without killing.
I break hearts and ruin lives.
I am cunning and malicious and gather strength with age.

The more I am quoted the more I am believed.
I flourish at every level of society.

My victims are helpless.
They cannot protect themselves against me because I have no
name and no face.

To track me down is impossible.
The harder you try, the more elusive I become.
I am nobody's friend.
Once I tarnish a reputation, it is never the same.
I topple governments and ruin marriages.
I ruin careers and cause sleepless nights, heartache and
indigestion.
I spawn suspicion and generate grief.

I make innocent people cry in their pillows.
Even my name hisses.

I AM CALLED GOSSIP!

Throughout the years I've seen many relationships fail because of gossip. There are some who act as if words do not hurt, then later find themselves bitter and sad, because they allowed gossip to destroy their confidence, morale, and self-esteem. I don't know about you, but gossip has always been a part of the juicy news around schools, in the media, and generally coming out of people's mouths. I have participated in gossip numerous times, and if there is one thing I'd want to take back, it is that. I've hurt several innocent people just because I spread rumors that were not true. Trust me, if you haven't felt the wrath of gossip, if you keep using it, it could be the same thing that comes back to hurt you. Remember, whatever we put out comes back on us doubled.

Words are capable of causing damage to us all no matter what age, race, or background. For example, let's say that you have a friend with whom you have been close for some years now, and one day another friend starts spreading a very bad rumor about you and blames it on your close friend. Let's say the rumor was not even true. Ask yourself, how you would feel before you even got a chance to ask your best friend about it?

My guess is that you would feel mad, sad, hurt, and vengeful. And that same thing is what has happened to all of us. I remember

74

a time during high school when a friend of mine started spreading lies about another guy in the school just because he was mad at him for something silly. To make a long story short, they both ended up fighting and being put out of school. Gossip destroys trust, and, most importantly, it destroys a willingness to trust new relationships that enter into our lives.

There are three main reasons for many of the relationships that will enter into our lives:

1. **Season** – These are the relationships that come into our lives, but fade away with time. A season is a period of time to learn and grow with a person and move on. Remember, if you ever want to test something, allow time to test it. Whatever stands the test of time will last.

2. **Reason** – I've met people in my life that I've only seen one time, but in one moment, I've learned something from them that has never left me.

3. **Lifetime** – These are the relationships that will always be around. These relationships/friendships are the ones you can count on for support, encouragement, and wisdom. They are positive in your life for as long as you live.

I have a very close friend of mine that is like a brother to me, and I value his friendship for the long haul.

Many times, when we try to hold on to relationships/friendships that were only meant for a season, they end up hurting us in the long run. I don't know about you, but I've had friends that I knew I wasn't supposed to be around. They were a bad influence in my life, but I held on anyway. When we had our disagreements and gossiped about each other, it made matters worse. When relationships are destroyed because of gossip, it creates a pain inside of us that lowers our trust level for new relationships that can benefit us. If you really understand the power of words, you'll know that someone else's negative comments can really hurt you.

The root of gossip

I've found out that the main reason why we gossip is so we do not focus on "self." The more we focus on someone else's failure, the better we feel about our own flaws. Gossip makes all our insecurities secure again. It gives us a false sense of freedom. It makes us feel that others are under our personal egos. We also sometimes gossip to invite people into our pity parties. We get out all of our anger and frustration through gossiping and talking down about someone else. It numbs all the pain we feel. We want others on our team so we can feel better about life. Then our friends repeat the story to their friends and on and on it goes. Even if you tell the truth, it does not justify the unnecessary passing on of hurtful information about someone else.

The feelings of gossip

There are several feelings that gossip will produce if we are not careful, and they can become addictive. Gossip produces pleasure, popularity, hurt, and blame. You have to be careful about what words you are using and whether you are spreading the truth or false information.

1. **Pleasure** – It produces pleasure because it makes us feel good inside that we know something about someone else. As long as it is not about us, if it is bad news we are happy. We have to watch this, because one day the bad news that is being spread could be about us.

2. **Popularity** - It produces a false sense of popularity. We feel popular when we know the latest dirt on someone else and people seek us out to find out what it is. We have to be careful about this, because we don't want to be known for the wrong things or for having the wrong information.

3. **Hurt** – Gossip produces hurt. We must always research to find out if something is true or not. We could be spreading lies on someone who has sunk so low that they want to

76

commit suicide or a violent crime. When we are on the receiving end of the gossip, it can disconnect us from people and mainly ourselves.

4. **Blame** – Gossip will have us feeling as though we have to participate in it, because we have been hurt in the past, so why not have someone else hurt, too? We have to avoid this, because it causes the victim complex, and will have you treating all people as if they are out to get you. We must remove the blame.

Getting rid of gossip

I have comprised a simple acronym for the word "gossip," and how we should use it to avoid gossip. For some, not gossiping may be easy, and for others it may be hard. But we need to understand the end results from using it.

- **G**et something positive in your mouth - Always say something good about people. You never know how you can impact someone's life or will need those same positive words someday yourself. Never put yourself into a position of needing the words or hand you didn't give.

- **O**nly take in good - Sometimes we get so caught up in only taking in the juicy negative gossip that we program our minds to block out the good around us. Take in the good for a change, and the next time someone shares gossip with you, respond with something good you have taken in.

- **S**pend time encouraging others - If you spend time encouraging others, you'll have no time to spread rumors. Remember, a rumor is how wars and battles start. I challenge you to encourage five to seven people a day, and see how many people look up to you.

- **S**peak life - Anytime someone gossips about you, always keep your character. Speak something positive to yourself. Never believe the negative statements of others about yourself, because if you do, your belief in the negative statement will have you acting that way.

- **I**nspire someone – Inspire someone else not to gossip. Gossip will never die as long as it has participants. Spread the news about how gossip destroys relationships. And remember never to get discouraged if others don't follow you from the beginning. Everyone must start from the ground up.

- **P**ace yourself - Don't try to change the world in a day. Not everyone will agree with your thoughts about being positive, but as you pace yourself you will find people whom you will inspire. I encourage you to do as much as you can, but never allow it to stress you or cause you to stop. Pace yourself.

Or, if you are the one who loves to gossip, I challenge you to take your words through this simple test. It is called the "THINK" test. My pastor, a well-read and extremely practical man, found the following acrostic and shared it with our congregation:

THE GOSSIP TEST

T – Is it true? Ask yourself, is what I'm about to say true?
H – Is it helpful? Ask yourself, is what I'm about to say helpful?
I – Is it inspiring? Ask yourself, is what I'm about to say inspiring?
N – Is it necessary? Ask yourself, is what I'm about to say necessary?
K – Is it kind? Ask yourself, is what I'm about to say kind?

If any of your thoughts or words fails this simple test, then just don't say it, and don't gossip.

Chapter 12

Anger 911:
How Anger Can Ruin Your Future

~

"If something has angered you, the only way to overcome it is to let it go now."

~*Terence B. Lester*

"Anger is what makes a clear mind seem clouded."

~*Kazi Shams*

"Anger not only separates us from people; it separates us from ourselves."

~*Terence B. Lester*

Of all the negative emotions that we feel as human beings, anger has to be one of the most destructive forces. It can totally change our personality and cause us to lose control of our behavior completely. First, let's define anger. Exactly what is anger?

I found the following statement on a popular online counseling web site.

"Simply put, anger is an emotion like all other emotions. Emotions are those feelings in our internal structure. It's simply something we feel."

----www.Allaboutcounseling.com

Growing up, I had a lot of internal anger, and, instead of finding a way to channel it, I acted it out in different ways. I'm here to tell you, it's not the anger that creates violence, but rather our choice to be angry. We all know that the word "anger" is one letter short of "danger," but let me tell you that, in a split-second, anger can rob your whole life. I remember a time when I became so angry that I became violent. I used my fist to knock out a window. The window belonged to the home of a person I did not know. Consequently, I could have gone to jail. If I had gotten caught and the person had pressed charges, I probably would have wasted valuable time in jail for getting upset over something that would not have meant very much to my future. I also caused damage to property of someone who was not connected in any way to the circumstances that made me lose control. If anger is not controlled, it can ruin a person and rob them of their future. Our anger must not hurt innocent people.

What can I do when I'm feeling angry?

There are several things you can do when you get upset and angry. One thing that I love doing is to turn my negatives into positives by writing. You may have a sport or a game that you enjoy playing. Whatever it is, I suggest that you involve yourself in such an activity until you cool off. Anger is not the emotion that produces the best reactions. You can even think through things that are bothering you, whether right or wrong, and try to find a reasonable solution. Think through what your basic feelings are. Take a "time-out" break. Remember, anger is a feeling that is here today, gone tomorrow, but the pain and repercussions we inflict on others may last a lifetime.

Many psychologists would argue that all anger begins with blame. We become angry at something. It isn't always easy to work out exactly what we're angry about, but that doesn't mean it isn't inside your heart. Usually, the focus of our anger is obvious, but, in some cases, it takes work to identify the exact root of our angry feelings. Most forms of counseling or mentoring are helpful here. We can apply blame three ways:

1. **The man or woman in the mirror** – This type of blame is what we call guilt and leads to depression.

2. **The first person we see** – This type of blame can result in many forms of anger, as well as unhealthy relationships.

3. **Anything above our heads** – This is anything that we cannot control, like rules, the law, or systems that are set in place.

Many people are walking around today angry. Many people are causing themselves to suffer from unresolved anger and other emotions. Unconsciously, some of us are still stuck in the past.

80

Past relationships, family/friends drama, memories, hurts, and traumas that have happened some time ago because of deep-rooted anger – all of these hold us in the grip of anger. Many of us do not take responsibility for our pain and feelings; therefore, we put the blame on those we feel have wronged us. As long as we blame others, we will never be able to let go and move on from pain and hurt.

You are not able to heal yourself until you realize that you are responsible for "making it right." You are the only one who can heal yourself with the help of God. Even though others may do things to hurt or offend you, you always have the power to determine how you let it affect you, how you decide to grow, and how you decide to learn from the situation(s).

If you believe that people will always let you down, you will always get let down. We attract those things in life that we believe to be true. If we want to stop feeling all of this hurt and anger all the time, we must change our way of thinking because our thoughts control our life. You determine how happy you are in life by your outlook on life. If all we think about are the negative things, we will never see the positive things.

We must learn to forgive others when they wrong us, even if we never forget. We must train our minds to think of the positive and not the negative. We must think of the future and let go of the past. You cannot change the past, but you can change your future. Let things go, and you will grow and leave anger behind.

If we can't get past the heavy baggage that we are carrying along and forgive past memories, we will truly be disappointed. If we want to stop feeling stressed, angry, depressed, and lonely, we must "let go and let God" move us to our next destination. If you go to the oven and pick up a pan with no gloves on, the pain will be too hot for you to carry it; so you have to let it go. Let go of those hot things in your life.

Even a flower must let go to grow. If not, it would always be a seed. You determine how happy or sad you are by a simple thought. Thoughts are more than wondering; they are the remotes to our picture. I guarantee you if we start to think more about the future instead of the past, we will move on and leave the past where it cannot follow. Remember, "Let things go and grow." We must clear the runway of everything in our lives that prohibits us from taking off and soaring to our destiny. Now, let's do a quick review:

Things that I should let GO

1. Negative past circumstances
2. Mistakes and unpleasant experiences
3. Ex-WHATEVER

The Process: When, How and Why?

I listen intently as my pastor teaches the Word of God. He often shares how important it is to let things go. He even has a three–step process that I call the "When-How-Why Plan." This is what he has taught me in regards to knowing how to let go:

WHEN: NOW.
HOW: BY ANY MEANS NECESSARY.
WHY: BECAUSE YOU ARE DESTINED FOR GREATNESS.

Life is full of choices, and the consequences for the choices you make. You never know what the outcomes will be whether, good or bad; accept them as learning tools to continue your journey. Can you control anger? Of course you can. It may take a little time; however, you were not created to be an angry and unhappy person. You are created in God's image. This means that you are a creature of peace, blessings and love.

I believe that all anger can be controlled. In fact, the anger I used to have is now channeled through my writing and speaking. No, I don't write harsh things or speak negative things; I use the energy and turn it into positive writing that will be a blessing to someone. If you find yourself getting upset and angry, here are some ways you can overcome anger:

1. **Count the cost** – Take time to think if it is really worth the consequences that you will receive as a result of your choices.

2. **Be a soft rock** – Express your feelings without hurting others with hard words.

3. **Eliminate blaming** – Look first in the mirror to see what "self" can do before you blame.

4. **Reward yourself with positive words** – Pat yourself on the back when you feel as though you have avoided negative situations.

5. **Release the air** – Anger comes from misunderstandings. Talking can release tension and give you new perspectives you haven't discovered. Find someone you can talk to, and not just anyone. Someone you can trust.

6. **Sweat it out** – Find something you can do to take your mind off of the problem. Even if it is playing a game that causes you to do physical exercise. Studies have shown that exercise releases anger and stress.

7. **Write down your thoughts** – This will release anger, so it will not continue to internalize negative thoughts.

Turning a negative into a positive

Here is a negative situation that I experienced. I was able to turn it into a positive once I got home and started to write about it.

The day seemed really downhill for me. It seemed like everything that I attempted was being bombarded with disappointing outcomes. I really felt like I was in a place where no one could feel my heart's pain, except for God. I mean, everything was being troubled. From relationships with close friends, to car trouble, to problems with finances, everything that came my way seemed not to have an attainable resolution.

How many of you know that there are millions of people living day-to-day feeling like their lives have been bombarded with similar circumstances? That's why I believe there are times like these when God will use pain as an invitation for us to trust and lean on him even more.

Well, as my day came near close, the last place I was going was to church before I returned home. So I went and enjoyed the service very much; but honestly, sometimes when you hurt so much it makes it hard to hear what God is trying to tell you, especially if your focus is on your hurt.

Well, as I was leaving the church, I misplaced my keys. This upset me even more. "What?" I yelled silently inside to God. "What are you trying to show me?" I yelled with anger. Earlier during the day things happened to me; now I can't find my keys. "What God? Please speak to me," I said. I looked all over for those keys, but found nothing. It got to the point where I just got fed up and sat on my car, frustrated.

Frustration is a place where the devil wants us. Do you know that no matter what the circumstance is, when we get frustrated we become stagnated and our focus becomes either distracted or destroyed? My mom always told me that no matter how much you get riled up, when you calm down, you still have to face your same circumstances.

As I sat there on that car and entertained my frustration, the situation got worse, simply because my focus wasn't where it was supposed to be. How many of you know that when you're not focused on what God has destined for your life, your focus will not be complete or whole? It will become what I now call a "keyless focus."

A keyless focus produces frustration, and frustration may lead us to stray from our purpose.

It was Harry Emerson Fosdick who said, "No steam or gas drives anything until it is confined. No life ever grows great until it is focused, dedicated, and disciplined."

While sitting on that car, something on the inside of me started to answer my questions. Those frustrations that I felt earlier, up to this point of losing my keys, were answered by a voice that simply said, "The keys are on you."

"The keys are on you," I said over and over. "What does that mean?" I asked myself. So I started to feel around in my pockets, and, to my surprise, the keys were right there all the time.

The whole time, the keys had been on me, but because I had so much stuff in my pocket, I could not feel the keys when I looked the first time. And just like life, we have so much stuff on us hurting us and bringing pain. We can't feel the keys and principles God put on and in front of us. This particular incident sparked a little voice inside of me that kept saying, "Don't let the devil fool you." I encourage you to follow the advice of the little voice. Don't be fooled by the devil and become angry. You will not be able to think as clearly as you normally would.

I believe God is telling us the same thing. I believe His voice would say the same thing, "Don't let the devil fool you. What I put on and in you can never be taken, but only covered up by your frustrations."

I'm here to tell you today that if you feel that you're not moving because your keys aren't there, before you become angry and ruin what could be a good day and a wonderful life, remember what happened to me. Your keys are already on you. If you are angry and feel like the world is against you, the keys are on you. If you feel like you don't know how, when or where, the keys are on you.

The dictionary defines "key" as an instrumental or deciding factor, or something that gives an explanation or identification or provides a solution.

I just want to let you know that God has put keys in each of us to unlock any door that may be closed. This includes the keys to dealing with anger. Any time a situation seems like it can't be opened, we must remember that we have the keys and power of God within us. And He is instrumental, or the deciding factor. I want to encourage you and say to you whatever you may be going through, "Hold on," because the keys are on you and in you. Whenever I feel locked down, I now look within for the keys God put in me to set me free. See, there are many things that we can do to relieve the stresses of life from hurting us. Today and right now, please find something that will help you release your anger and turn your life around.

Chapter 13

Peer Pressure: Seven Signs of Peer Pressure

~

"If you allow peer pressure to make all your decisions, when you receive the consequences, life will have no time to listen to your excuses."
~Terence B. Lester

In this life, there are many things that can distract us from doing the things that we really need to do. Sometimes we connect with the wrong friends, find ourselves moving toward the wrong location or work toward the wrong pursuits. All these things can become detrimental to our lives. Growing up, as I told you before, I dealt with a lot of peer pressure. I understand how it becomes so easy to listen to friends versus listening to your parents. I'm here to tell you that if peers are pressuring you negatively and it is causing you concern or alarm, you should tell someone. I remember in middle school that I was pressured into being in the local gang. I knew that I didn't want to become a part of it, but, sometimes when all your friends are saying things and you feel like no one understands, it can leave you open to be pressured. I want to disclose both to the parent and the child the seven signs of peer pressure and how they affected me.

1. **Secrets** – This is one of the biggest signs of peer pressure. Not only did I hide a lot of the peer pressure growing up, it hurt me in a lot of ways. The signs of hiding can often be found in quick answers, nonchalant attitudes and smart comments. From my own experiences, I truly understand that a lot of things that I was hiding were simply because I felt like an adult wouldn't understand. Since this world is set up to prejudge people based on their past instead of what they can become, it stops a lot of children from opening up to their parents. This is not because the parent is bad, but because the world has programmed us to think this way. If you are sensing that your child is hiding something, or if you are a child who's hiding something, stop. I've had

too many failures in trying to deal with things myself. It's when we seek help that we avoid the painful experiences.

2. **Isolation and privacy** – Too much privacy allowed me to try new things. I was raised in a household without a father around and my mom was at work most of the time. So guess what? I had to raise myself a little, and, trust me; I wasn't very good at it. Sometimes when there is too much time on our hands, we can end up listening to the wrong people. I encourage you to get involved in some extra-curricular activities that are positive, activities that will help you in your future. Parents, if you ever feel that you don't get to spend enough time with your child, please do so. I got into more trouble without supervision than I did with it.

3. **Covering up for friends** – I had a lot of friends and was well known by a lot of my peers, but that wasn't the problem. The problem started when I would tell my mom how good someone was when he or she really wasn't. As I look back now, a lot of the trouble I faced came from hanging with the wrong people at the wrong time. If you are covering up for someone that you know will hinder your future, stop. Parents, if you suspect your child is hanging with people who are not good, then, more than likely, they are. Parents, don't choose your child's friends; they have to understand this process on their own. Instead, teach them the importance of choosing their friends wisely. Hanging with the wrong people is bad news and will stop their progress in life if they continue. Young people, I'm not saying cut off all your friends, I'm simply saying, know your friends and how they will help or hinder your progress.

4. **Weird behavior** – This is another sign of peer pressure. I started acting differently when I hung around the wrong people. If you know your child well, you will know that the change in your child's behavior is not indicative of how you raised them. Then more than likely they are hanging

around the wrong people. Young people, never let anyone change who you are. Here is a keynote: if you have to change the way you act around people, then they are not your friends.

5. **Change in personality** – A change in personality is also a good sign that there is peer pressure in the picture. When I say, "change in personality," I'm not talking about what they do differently; I'm talking about actually becoming who they are trying to be. I became a person who I wasn't raised to be because of the crowd I followed. When you allow peer pressure to change who you actually are, then you need to talk with someone about this before it messes up your life. I have too many old friends in prison, on drugs, or dead. I also have friends who had straight As and Bs, and, once they got out of high school, their lives headed down the wrong path, hanging around the wrong crowd after they left their parents' house. Young people, never change who you are. There might be times you change what you do, but never let anyone change who you are.

6. **Involvement in trouble** – Continuously getting into trouble is another sure sign of peer pressure. If you are a parent, you can tell if your child is being pressured by the frequency and type of trouble they may encounter. A lot of times, I got into trouble that wasn't even in my character, but, because I changed who I was as a person, it changed the type of trouble I encountered. A lot of times when you are doing things that don't reflect your character, you need to talk it over with someone who understands how to point you in the right direction. Some types of trouble include: fights, drug use, being angry at everyone, and rebellious behavior towards adults.

7. **Bad locations/hangouts** – These are the places that teens go that they wouldn't normally go. If you ask to go places where you know your parents wouldn't let you go, then its peer pressure. So many wrong things can happen in the wrong place at the wrong time. I had a friend who lost his

life in high school, not because he was a bad person, but because he was in the wrong place at the wrong time, with the wrong people. There are so many things that can happen in the wrong location. I have been in so much trouble because of being in the wrong place at the wrong time. Please, whatever you do, protect yourself from being in the wrong place at the wrong time.

These are situations that you can find yourself involved in even though you did not have any intentions of participation: bank robberies, car jacking, fighting, cutting class, driving drunk, and other activities that are harmful and can lead to a police record. Let me share an example. There was a young man in southwest Atlanta. He was from a good family, and lived with his mother and father in one of the nicer areas of the city. His parents had every reason to trust him.

One day, he was walking up the street, and a few of his friends came along in a car. They asked him if he wanted to ride. He said that he did and got into the car. His parents had told him not to get into cars with other teenagers unless he had prior approval. About three blocks further up the street, he heard sirens and saw the blue lights of a police car. Before these young guys picked him up they had gone to a high school in another county and stolen some things from cars in the parking lot, among them a nice boom-box radio. The owner reported the theft and probably gave them a tag number of the vehicle. Anyway, they were pulled over.

He had just gotten in the car, but was taken to jail. His parents were forced to get a lawyer and pay a lot of money to see to it that he had legal counsel during the trial. He was guilty of simply getting into the car with other young men who did not have the same values that he had. They had stolen from others, and he was charged just as they were. He never forgot that he had not followed his parents' instructions never to get in the car and joy-ride with other teenagers, unless he had permission first. Just like he was pressured, you will find yourself in the same situation. The question is, what will you do? How will you handle peer pressure?

How to handle those who are pressuring you

If you are being pressured to do something that you don't want to do, talk it over and explain to the person who is pressuring you that you are not interested. If that doesn't work, stop going around that person, and seek professional support.

Whom can I talk to about it?

You can talk to a mentor, counselor, parent, brother, sister, or whoever will give you good advice.

Atmosphere and Environment

You have to understand that whatever atmosphere or environment you put yourself in will determine your temperament (attitude and outcome) and what you get involved with. In our daily actions, I believe that we have to have careful thinking. I will explain this.

There are times when we get beside ourselves. We get down and worry at the feet of defeat. Don't give up. The roughest times brought upon us are the very experiences that will make us grow stronger in our faith. These experiences are nourishment that will help us grow and bring us closer to purification. The enemy wants to see you hang your head. Don't give up. Through your trials of judgment, don't give up. The ultimate and final verdict will be rewarding. When we worry, we are saying that we don't trust God. We make the little problem bigger and forget about all the big things God has already done for us.

Learn to look at what you do have, not what you don't have. God may not create or cause every bad situation, but he can and will turn every situation around for the good. "And we know that all things work together for good to those who love God, to those who are called according to his purpose" (Romans 8:28 NKJV). Even if we lose faith in ourselves and mankind, we should never lose faith in God.

I have put together an acronym for the word CAREFUL because I believe that we need to be careful in our thinking.

C – Character – Our character defines who we are through our actions. Our character determines how we are and how we will always be. Our character is the definition of our heart. In order to have a great character, we must find ourselves; in finding ourselves we become more confident of who we are and whose we are. We must have great character to become confident, productive citizens.

A – Affiliations – Everything you surround yourself with is a reflection of you. Everything around you can affect you. If you are around negativity, eventually you will turn negative and destroy your character. We should always be aware of our affiliations. It is better to be alone, than in wrong company.

R – Respect – If you respect God, you'll respect yourself. And by respecting yourself, you will be able to respect others. Respect strengthens and defines your character, and disrespect will ruin your character. You must have respect to be able to get to your respected destination in life.

E – Entertainment – The things that entertain you are the things that hold your attention and focus; your attention and focus are what build your future. Hard work and preparation towards the destination prepare you for the future. If negative things are included in your daily entertainment, then they will be the roots of your spirit; if you entertain the things that will promote positive movement through your spirit, you will attract a positive outcome.

F – Focus – Focus on what is important. When you stay focused, your vision becomes clearer. You have to stay focused on wherever you are headed in life. If you are not focused, you might go off track completely. This also builds discipline for your character, affiliations, respect, and your choices for the environment of your entertainment. Always stay focused, and have a clear vision of your future.

U – Understanding – If you are an understanding and forgiving person, it will eliminate a lot of evil things and stress in your life. Understanding is having a clear, peaceful mind and seeing two views at all times. This will help you relate to people and life positively.

L – Location – Location is the most important point of this acronym, because, if you are in the wrong location at the wrong time, how will you receive the right things at the right time? If you are setting out to be anything, you have to know that the right location is necessary for your success. Whoever places themselves in the wrong locations will destroy their destination.

I believe that with careful thinking you will be careful in everything that God places in your mind. If you carefully think of peaceful living, you'll be at peace.

DISCOVERING THE WILL AND THE WAY

Chapter 14

Dealing with Loneliness

~

"Loneliness is isolation with a purpose."
~ *Terence B. Lester*

"Being lonely doesn't always mean something is wrong with you."
~ *Terence B. Lester*

Feeling Lonely?

I would dare say that everyone probably experiences loneliness at some point in life. During my teenage years, I hung around a lot of people. There was always a crowd of people following me. Even with all of these people around, there still were times that I felt very lonely. I discovered that just because you are in a crowd, it doesn't mean that you can't feel lonely. I learned so much from that experience, because it showed me that it's not the people you are hanging around that make you the person you are, it's finding out who you are inside. I remember many times laughing, joking, and playing with my friends, while in the back of my head, I was thinking, "I'm all alone."

What I found out was that growth and change during teenage years produce a lot of different feelings inside. Loneliness is not always necessarily being alone. We may be alone for long periods without feeling lonely at all. On the other hand, we may feel lonely in a familiar setting without really understanding why. As I mature, when I look back, I understand the loneliness that I felt came because there was something in me longing to find "me." I mean I had to get to a point where I knew who I was. When you don't know who you are, anyone will be able to influence you. That's why we have to focus on building up who we are as individuals. The best way to begin to understand loneliness is to examine some of the ways we experience it. We many feel lonely when:

- We feel like there is something missing inside.

97

- Our parents and friends don't seem to understand our personal pains and hurts.
- Our teachers accuse us and don't want to hear our side.
- We feel something in the past that hurts us today.
- Changes: a new school, a new state, teacher, friends, or physical changes.
- We feel that there's no one in our life with whom we can share our inner thoughts and feelings, or that no one understands us, period.
- Our view of self is a lack of confidence. We feel neglected, unacceptable, belittled, and that we are not worthwhile.

A lot of people have many misconceptions and myths about loneliness. Many people feel that loneliness is a sign of weakness or immaturity, or that there's something wrong with them if they are lonely. They think that if they are lonely, they're lost, or that they are the only one who feels that way. If you believe these myths about feeling lonely and that something is wrong in your personality, you are wrong. "Whoever you think you are, you're right." When I believed that something was wrong with me for feeling lonely, I started feeling like I didn't fit. I realized that I had hard times making new friends, encouraging others, participating in groups, and in enjoying myself at parties or functions.

When we believe that something is wrong with us, the results might be that we end up feeling depressed, angry, afraid, and misunderstood. There were plenty of times when I felt lonely, and as a result I thought something was wrong with me. Little did I know that God was trying to show me who I was in Him. A lot of people experience loneliness, not because they are alone, but because they are still searching for who they really are. When you find out who you are in Christ Jesus, the loneliness goes away. If you are feeling lonely, there may be nothing wrong with you. You have to understand that something inside of you is searching to know why you even exist. I believe that you should pick your head up and start seeking to find out exactly who you are. So many of the friends that I got in trouble with when I was younger never grew to change their mind-set, not because they were ignorant, but because they never took time to find themselves.

What to do about loneliness

Feeling lonely is not the most sought-out feeling, and, since this emotion saddens us, we try to avoid it at all cost. The only way to change loneliness is to realize first who you are, and by doing that you can grow and become confident. Second, know that loneliness is not permanent. It is also important to know that loneliness is a common experience. Remember, everyone has felt a sense of loneliness at one point in time, even the greats.

Begin by identifying which needs are not being met in your specific situation, and why you are feeling lonely. Most times, we desire something to make us feel whole. Your loneliness may result from a variety of needs. It may involve the need to develop a circle of friends that will add to you instead of subtracting from you. It may even involve learning to do things for yourself or learning responsibilities without friends. Or it may involve learning to be more content and confident in what you do. During lonely times, I advise you to study yourself and watch how much stronger you become.

Taking time to develop yourself when you feel lonely

1. Think of yourself as a whole person. When I say "whole," I mean complete.

2. Take care of yourself where you begin to grow and know yourself. Know what makes you happy, what makes you mad, and what gives you peace.

3. Don't let the wrong friends, focus, or other interests cause you to become distracted from your main goal.

4. Use your "alone time" to get to know yourself. Find ways you can grow while you are alone. Read, watch interesting films, or just meditate about life.

5. Use your alone time to enjoy yourself. I always find new ways to enjoy my time alone. Some of my best ideas come to me when I'm at total silence and alone.

It wasn't until I was alone that I fully discovered my gifts of writing, speaking, and interest in encouraging others.

In conclusion, don't define yourself as a lonely person. No matter how bad you feel, loneliness will fade over time as you become more familiar with yourself. Remember, you are not alone. Many have felt how you are feeling. Always look at the positive in feeling that way, because you can find your gifts, talents, abilities, and purpose for living. That's how I found mine. Don't wait for your feelings to get you going – get going, and good feelings will eventually catch up with you.

Here is a really good poem by an unknown author that I like to read whenever I feel down or lonely:

START OVER

If you've started out in pursuit of your goal
And you've really tried with your heart and your soul,
But somehow things got out of control---
START OVER.

When you've tried your best to do what you should
And you thought this time that you surely would,
But once again, you didn't do good---
START OVER.

When you've worked so hard to follow the right way
And you fought to win a victory each day.
But one more time you went astray---
START OVER.

When you've tried so hard to yourself to be true
And do the things that you know you should do,
But once again you failed to come through---
START OVER.

When the road to success seemed much too long
And each temptation was oh so strong
And once again you gave in to wrong---
START OVER.

When you've told your friends what you planned to do
And trusted them to help you through
But soon discovered it's up to you---
START OVER.

When you know you must be physically fit,
But your hope seems gone and you're stuck in a pit
That's not the time for you to quit---
START OVER.

When the week seems long and successes few
And at weigh-in time you're feeling blue,
Remember tomorrow is just for you---
START OVER.

To start again means a victory's been won
And starting over again means a race well run
And starting over again proves it can be done
So don't just sit there---
START OVER.

-Author Unknown

Chapter 15

Opening Up Will Help You

~

"A single conversation across the table with a
wise man is better than ten years' study of books."
~Chinese Proverb

"Talking lets the hot air out."
~Terence B. Lester

Sometimes when life becomes difficult, people tend to close up and go off by themselves. This helps to contribute to the loneliness syndrome. It is much better to find someone in whom you can confide and express what you are going through. There are many conflicts in life. I have shared already that many times these conflicts begin deep within. It is during these times that you must concentrate on "inner conflict resolution."

Inner-Conflict Resolution

Opening up is one of the greatest ways to express yourself and clear up a lot of the things that bother you internally and externally. One form of opening up is conflict resolution. Conflict resolution has helped me in the past, and it still helps me today. First of all, let's find out what conflict resolution happens to be. One of the best ways to do that might be to find out what it is not. If you are faced with problems, personal or public, the following will not resolve these issues:

1.   Holding on to the problem.
2.   Surrounding yourself with people that thrives on conflict.
3.   Thinking about negative things to do.
4.   Not talking it out.
5.   Holding grudges.

These things neither resolve conflict(s), nor help in any other way. I remember, one time I had gotten so upset because I couldn't have my way in a certain situation. Well, I came across a wise lady who told me something that I would like to share with you. She said, "If you are mad now, it won't change the situation for the future." That lady was my mom. I wanted to go somewhere, but I had gotten in trouble at school the previous week. Years later, I agree with my mom. If you are mad about something, let it go, because it's not important or healthy to hold on to negativity. I want you to know that I understand when you say, "Nobody understands me." I'm here to tell you, there are people who understand, and I am one of them.

Let's talk Conflict Resolution

Most resolution experts would argue that "conflict is a normal aspect of human interaction that often arises from unmet needs, unrecognized differences, and difficulties coping with life changes. Conflict can either produce positive or negative results depending on the communication techniques used." I totally agree with them. When you usually hear of conflict resolution, you hear about two or more people getting involved in a heated argument or disagreement. My question is, what do you do when you have a conflict with yourself?

What will you do when you get to the point where you are about to give up? I've been to the point where I wanted to give up several times, but when I started opening up, I slowly but surely resolved the conflict that I had within myself. There are so many people walking around who don't even like themselves simply because they hold everything in and never release what is inside of them. They start to have what I call "curse words." No, not the type of curse words called "profanity," but the curse words that will keep you from moving forward in life, achieving goals, and, most importantly, resolving your inner conflict.

Let me show you the curse words that I'm referring to and how they will keep you from solving the problems you are dealing with inside. Here are the curse words you should look out for and the things you should say when you hear them:

Curse Words	Replacing Curse Words
I can't	I can

I don't believe	I am a true believer
I'm not worthy	I am worthy
I quit	I'll work harder
I give up	I will not give up
I'll try	I will accomplish
I wish	I will have
I'm not good enough	I am the best I can be
I don't know anything	I will learn what I don't know
I'm a loser	I'm a winner by faith
I want that dream	I will own that dream
I can never see myself	I can see myself reaching any goal that I envision

The way to break out of the habit of cursing yourself is simply thinking positively. Positive thoughts kill negative words. There are many times we use curse words without actually cursing. A true curse word is a word that leaves your mouth and robs your power of achieving. It also leaves an invisible brick in front of you every time you use one of these words. Some people use these words so much that the bricks build a wall and they hide themselves behind their curse words. Remember, curse words are the words you use against yourself and your own ability.

Thinking positively is a good tool for resolving conflict when you are faced with problems that are bothering you internally. Let me share a story that I heard an inspirational speaker share on peace, because in order to solve problems, have good inner conflict resolution, or get over your problems, you should seek peace.

It was the third year at the paint-off, where painters from across the world would come and paint portraits for cash prizes. This year's theme was "peace" and there were only two finalists who made it to the championship. One artist was an older gentleman who was known for winning many championships, and the other guy was a homeless man that happened to make it as a special entry.

As they set out to paint a picture pertaining to "peace," each artist was sent to the same spot. They were set up in front of a pretty house on a hill with bright sunshine, a lake, some doves, a stream, ducks, a swing, and a big oak tree with a bird happily sitting on a branch, singing. The older gentleman painted the picture just as he saw it. He painted a pretty house on a hill with bright sunshine, a lake, some doves, a stream, ducks, a swing, and a big oak tree with a bird happily sitting on a branch, singing.

The homeless man painted a totally different picture. It contained the same objects, only the portrait he painted looked as if a great storm had just passed by. The sky was dark, the house was old, rusty, and cracked, the lake was greenish-looking, the ducks were gone, the swing had blown over, and the oak tree was tipped over with the bird still sitting on a branch, singing.

Each of the painters returned to see who would win the prize and, after reviewing both pictures, the homeless man won with the stormy-looking picture. The older guy was furious. He ran up to the judges and screamed, "How could he have won? My picture was pretty, precise, straight to the point, and had peace."

"Yeah." said the head judge, "but in this guy's picture, even though his house was bad, the sky was dark, the swing had tipped over, the lake was green, and the oak tree was knocked over in the storm, the bird was still singing during all of that."

The moral of the story is that "peace is not always what it looks like, but how it feels in spite of what it looks like." So no matter what's going on in your life, there is always an internal resolution called "peace." That's how I made a 360° turnaround from being angry to having peace. I looked for peace.

Here are some other ways to resolve your inner conflicts:

1. **Admit there is a problem**. The very first step in dealing with any problem is to acknowledge that there is a problem.

2. **Recognize that God is the only real source that can restore you fully**. You do not have to do it alone. Find someone to open up to and release the things that bother you. Surrendering to the fact that you can't control this alone is a good way to become proactive instead of reactive. You can go to mentors, peer managers, a coach, or even a youth pastor to discuss the issues, but always it is God who will fully restore you and give you joy.

U Turn

3. **Choose to turn it over**. Sometimes the biggest obstacle is you. There are times when the best thing you can do is get out of the way and let God make you into who you are supposed to become.

4. **Analyze the situation to determine the cause.** Where did you drop the ball or how could you have handled the situation differently? Remember, if it begins with you, it can end with you.

5. **Create a successful plan of action with another person**. An objective view eliminates blind spots and also brings attention to what we do not see ourselves. This step must be taken with someone with integrity who is concerned about both your future and your growth.

6. **Humbly get into action**. Become a servant, and start doing things for others, and see how much better you feel. Giving is one of the biggest stress-relievers for me.

7. **Lead by example**. Show up as a leader who can solve personal, inner conflicts and help others overcome their own. After a while, people will go where you lead them, so lead by example.

Expressing yourself verbally heals silently

A lot of my healing started when I began to perform the poetry I was writing at the time. The first time I performed, I was a bit nervous. But after I got through it and heard the applause of the crowd, I began to gain confidence. This helped me to start the inner turnaround process. By opening up and releasing what was inside me, I was able to resolve and overcome a lot of inner conflict. If I had continued to hold on to all of the things that bothered me, I probably would have experienced some or most of the following:

1. It could have killed me, because stress causes death.

2. It could have prompted me to do something that could have cost me my life.
3. It could have caused me to continue to hurt people who love me.

Whenever you have a lot of conflict inside, try opening up in a way that will help you during your process of resolving inner conflict. It can be singing, dancing, or playing games, but I suggest that you talk with someone as well.

Here is the difference in forgetting an issue and forgiving yourself regarding an issue.

Forgetting and Forgiving

There is a big difference when it comes to forgetting and forgiving. We must understand that forgetting a thing is like burying treasure…it can be dug back up. But forgiveness is like pulling up the roots to a weed; it can never grow back again. Here are five things that can help you distinguish the difference between the two.

1. Forgetting the past risks that it can re-emerge to haunt you. Forgiving self from the past cuts out all negative thinking that can arise in the future.

2. Forgetting that a person hurt us is like deferred pain, because it can be brought back up to hurt us again. Forgiveness removes the future pain from memory.

3. Forgetting a mistake without learning from it produces procrastination. Forgiveness acknowledges that I messed up and that I'm going to grow from this situation.

4. Forgetting to focus can cause confusion. Forgiveness humbles us to the point where we understand that we cannot do anything without God.

5. Forgetting a wrong act produces an option to do it again. Forgiveness repents and changes the wrong act and the direction of our thinking.

We must understand that forgetting sin didn't set us free, forgiveness of sin did. Forgetting may set the soul loose for a moment, but forgiveness sets the soul free for a lifetime.

I remember receiving this message from a friend one day, and I believe that the questions written represented where "real life" meets "faith."

1. What do you do when all has gone wrong?
2. What do you do when you don't have the answers and can't find the answers?
3. What do you do when all your bills are due and you don't have the money for all of them?
4. What do you do when hope sometimes seems to be floating around, but you miss the target every time?
5. What do you do when your family and friends turn their backs on you?
6. What do you do when you have tithes, but don't have the late fee for your rent, then other times have the rent but no favor around you?
7. What do you do when you don't have any gas money or gas in the car?

What do you do?

This is the first thought that came to my mind as I read this message. When you're sick, nothing else matters but health. When you're alone, nothing else matters but companionship. When you're out of hope, nothing else matters but faith. When you're lost, nobody else matters but God. "In our weakest moments, we distinguish who means the most and what we take for granted."

Now I will share another story that a family member shared with me. One day, my cousin called me and told me that his close friend's mother had just committed suicide. He said that his friend had not spoken to her mother in one month and that they ended on a bad conversation. Five weeks later, the body of his friend's mother was found in her home where she had been dead for five weeks without anyone's noticing. When I think of this, all the things we consider problems seem very small when "life" is over.

The reason I speak on this topic is because this touched me in a very deep way. Whatever problems we may be facing in life are not that important when "life" is over. We have been given the best gift, which happens to be life itself, and relationships that mean something to us. How many times do we neglect the gifts God has granted us? So, I pose this question, "What do we do when life is over?"

All we can do is trust in the Lord with all our heart and lean not on our own understanding. We never know when our last day may come. We should live every day happy despite our bad situations. Material possessions are no match for the gift of life itself. God knows all our wants and needs and never puts us in a position that we can't handle. God gives us everything we need inside to make it out of the problems we face outside.

This day as you read this, cherish and celebrate the gift of life. Let's lift someone's spirit and love our family, simply because, when we don't know what to do, we have God, life, and the relationships He has trusted us with.

I thank God for "life," even when I don't know what to do next.

Today, cherish your life so much that you will address any problems and bring forth resolution to continue to move forward.

Chapter 16

Building/Rebuilding Bridges to Parents and Teachers

Help! My parents and teachers don't understand me.

~

"The eye sees only what the mind is prepared to comprehend."
~Henri Bergson

"Parents understand, just with age…LOL."
~Terence B. Lester

I wonder if there are any teenagers left who have not felt, at one time or another, that their parents simply did not understand them. As human beings, it is very important that we are understood. This validates our opinion and existence.

Why we need understanding

I've found throughout my life that we need to feel that we are active players in the game of life. We need to be listened to so that our feelings are taken into consideration. Most of all, we need to be heard. By receiving all the great things, we must first understand each other. During my life, as I felt like no one understood me, I can honestly say that everything that I remember that my mom said to me came true as I lived through the experiences of life. For example, let's say that you have a child and that child loves toys. You work a job that doesn't pay that much, but enough for you to survive. One day, you and your child go to the store. In the heat of the moment, your child sees a toy that he likes. Well, you're thinking in your mind, "I want to purchase the toy," but the child is thinking, "I have to have this toy." When you finally say, "No, you can't have the toy," without explaining how it would affect the household funds, the child feels like the parent doesn't understand how much they "need" the toy. This causes a conflict, because there are two opposing views: the parent is thinking of the future; the child is thinking for the moment.

111

This is what happens when there is a lack of understanding. We as young people only think for the moment, instead of seeing the big picture. When the child in the story grows up and is faced with the same problem as the parent, he or she would tell his or her child the same thing and use the same reasoning. Behind this whole story, we learn a valuable lesson and truth that happens to be, "Experience is the best teacher of understanding if you are not willing to listen." I believe that the only way for us to understand is to:

1. **Listen:** Actively listen to everything that is being said by either your parent or teacher. Get all the facts, and get a full understanding of what's going on. Listen to them fully and intensely.

2. **Switch roles:** Put yourself in their shoes and pretend that you are the adult and they are the child, and be honest about how you would handle the same situation.

This doesn't hurt and it helped me to see things from different perspectives. I like this quote by Van Gogh: "If one is master of one thing and understands one thing well, one has at the same time, insight into and understanding of many things." This is good insight and understanding.

Letting my guard down

Anytime that we don't feel like we are being understood, the first thing we should do is tear down the mental walls that we have built and stop complaining. Anytime we complain, we tear down our ability to build on anything inside. Complaining not only hurts us, it also affects our surroundings and viewpoints. People generally complain when their patience seems to be running thin or when one problem overwhelms them to the point that they take it out on everything around them. I believe complaining is the number one killer of happiness and joy. Complaining causes excuses, builds up a wall, and causes things, such as trying to understand, to be delayed. The only way to beat complaining is simply to weed out the negative thoughts. When negative thoughts come, we have to be aware always that there is a bright side.

Sometimes, when our thoughts go flat, we just have to pump them back up. This enables us to get back on track. When we complain about the small things, we remove and scare away the big things destined for our lives. Take care of little things, so you can be blessed with greater things. *"He who is Faithful in what is least is faithful also in much; and he who is unjust in what is least is unjust also in much"* (NKJV Luke 16:10).

It's both hard and hurtful when we get in places where we feel like no one understands us. Let me tell you that everyone won't understand you. I have been hurt so many times, because I expected everyone to understand what and how I felt. It wasn't until I realized who I was, whose I was, and my purpose for living that I stopped caring about what others thought.

This is something that I wrote one day when I was feeling like no one understood the pain that I was feeling.

Words in a Dark Place

"I'm running down a tunnel nobody knows; it's very dark and full of valleys and curves. If it were up to me, I would give up now; but something keeps calling my heart. I've been running for some time now, and I believe I'm lost. But since I can see a light at the end of the tunnel, I'm going to keep on running, hoping that one day soon, I may get to the light that's calling my name and heart. During my journey, I've fallen many times, I've been scared more than once, I've almost given up, and I've received many scars, but no one or no thing will stop me from reaching that light that's in my heart. Whether that light is purpose, whether that light is destiny, whether that light is desire and hunger, I will not stop, because God gave it to me. If the light is your goal, no tunnel is dark enough for you to stop persevering to the mark God gave you during pain."

I've learned that once a person becomes aware of reason and purpose, nothing and no one will ever be able to steal the cause in their heart. If you start focusing on where you want to go in life, feeling misunderstood won't bother you much. It was when I found my purpose for living that I stopped caring about being misunderstood and feeling neglected. I believe that there is a release in finding your purpose in life. I still feel misunderstood sometimes today, but it doesn't affect me, because I know where I am headed in life. Find your purpose and focus on where you're going.

Finding common ground

Another good way of getting your point across and being understood is to find common ground. Find a topic that relates and agrees; never attack. When we get in a defensive mode, it can cause us to shut down completely. The main objective is to grab hold of communication with whomever you feel doesn't understand you and work from there. It was Jason H. Thomas who observed, *"Being vulnerable and transparent is one of the hardest things in the world to do, but it's one of the best things that we can ever do."* Never bring negativity into a misunderstanding, because eventually both parties will misunderstand. If you have a situation now with anyone and feel like you're not being understood, find common ground or change the subject. Remember, misunderstanding is not our goal in life. Rather, it is to gain understanding. Our main goal is to learn from our past mistakes and grow. We are trying to turn our lives all the way around mentally, 360°, and not half-way.

Give and Receive

Another good way to avoid misunderstanding between you and your parent or teacher would be to do something nice, give help on something that needs to be done, or give a gift. One of the biggest teachings in the Bible is giving. Giving benefits you internally and it creates a bridge between you and whomever you don't feel understood by. I'm not saying to buy happiness or bribe anyone. I'm simply saying, give with your whole heart, and watch how much that begins to open doors for good communication.

This story was sent to me through email one day, and I believe it's a good lesson on giving. It is for the parent, teacher, child, and student. Too many times, we look at how our parents don't understand and how the children don't understand, and we end up missing the true meaning of life. Here is the story; it's called "Twenty Dollars per Hour."

Twenty Dollars per Hour

The man came home from work late again, tired and irritated, to find his five-year-old son waiting for him at the door. "Daddy, may I ask you a question?"

"Yeah, sure, what is it?" replied the man.

"Daddy, how much money do you make an hour?"

"That's none of your business! What makes you ask such a thing?" the man said angrily.

"I just want to know. Please tell me, how much do you make an hour?" pleaded the little boy.

"If you must know, I make $20.00 an hour."

"Oh," the little boy replied, head bowed. Looking up, he said, "Daddy, may I borrow $10.00 please?"

The father was furious. "The only reason you wanted to know how much money I make is just so you can borrow some to buy a silly toy or some other nonsense. March yourself straight to your room and go to bed. Think about why you're being so selfish. I work long, hard hours every day and don't have time for such childish games." The little boy quietly went to his room and shut the door. The man sat down and started to get even madder about the little boy's question. How dare he ask such questions only to get some money! After an hour or so, the man had calmed down and started to think he may have been a little hard on his son. Maybe there was something he really needed to buy with that $10.00, and he really didn't ask for money very often. The man went to the door of the little boy's room and opened the door. "Are you asleep, Son?" he asked.

"No, Daddy, I'm awake," replied the boy.

"I've been thinking, maybe I was too hard on you earlier," said the man. "It's been a long day and I took my aggravation out on you. Here's that $10.00 you asked for."

The little boy sat straight up, beaming, "Oh, thank you, Daddy!" he yelled. Then, reaching under his pillow, he pulled out some more crumpled-up bills. The man, since the boy already had money, started to get angry again. The little boy slowly counted out his money, then looked up at the man.

"Why did you want more money if you already had some?" the father grumbled.

"Because I didn't have enough, but now I do," the little boy replied. "Daddy, I have $20.00 now. Can I buy an hour of your time?"

~Unknown Author

If you feel like no one understands you, then start sharing time with that particular person by whom you would like to be understood. Then open up to them -- especially if it is a parent. No matter how it goes, always leave loved ones with loving words. It may be the last time you see them. Pray and ask God to open their heart to receive your true essence (who/what you really are) rather than how they have perceived you before. A lot of people miss out on the treasure of relationships, because they bury themselves under the past. Out of frustration, they close doors too soon. Time is best spent with someone you love. Don't let time steal your chance to love because of a simple misunderstanding. I encourage you to do your part and try to work it out.

Chapter 17

Comfort Zone Poem (What Will You Do?)

~

"If you stay in your comfort zone too long, it could set you up for failure."
~Terence B. Lester

I hope you are getting something worthwhile out of this guide. It takes making a full U-turn to see results. I want each one of you to succeed in life. I believe that you all are great people and winners, but it starts with application. You have to decide at this point that you will act on what you have read. Some of you will and some of you won't, but I want you to know that if you don't, life will teach you lessons. One of the best decisions I ever made in life was to change my mindset. Not halfway, but a 360° turnaround. If you are like me, I know that you will eventually change and have a very productive and successful life. Let me give you six points that will help you make your turnaround mentally:

60° – I think about doing something bad, I do it and get in trouble. It takes forever to get out of this mess. It's not my fault.

120° – I do the same things that got me in trouble before. It takes me even longer to get out of trouble. It's not my fault.

180° – I get in trouble again for the same old thing. It's becoming a habit. It is my fault, and I understand that it's my fault.

240° – I think before I do those things that get me in trouble. I'm learning to think my way out trouble before it happens.

300° – I am tempted by my old habits, but I'm searching for a way to avoid them totally.

360° – I U-turn, change my thinking completely, and head my life in a different direction.

I want to share this poem entitled, "Comfort Zone," which I wrote years back when God was calling me to dig deeper in writing:

Comfort Zone – "Step Out"

I used to have a "comfort zone," where I knew I couldn't fail.

It's amazing how sometimes the walls of our minds, can box us up like jails.

I always thought about things that I wanted to do but I stayed inside my "comfort zone"…on first base, and never went for TWO.

I often tried to hide all the pain of never stepping out, but a little small voice inside my heart said, "You can do it" with a determined shout.

It told to me "something is in you, but you'll never know how much if you stay comfortable."

So, I started getting restless because I was very anxious, and my passion built up and provoked my thinking.

That voice in my heart whispered "think a little deeper and start to sow seeds and soon you'll be reaping."

So day after day, I thought as deep as I could, until my mind started seeing pass the bad, realizing the good.

So I got my pen and paper and wrote what was in my heart, suddenly a fire ignited and purpose began to spark.

And before I knew it I was completely out of the zone, because I followed the voice in my heart and left my "comfort zone."

Sometimes we fool ourselves and give excuses saying we're too busy,

Not knowing that "only" talking wastes more time than productivity.

I couldn't let my life go by just watching others win.
Because I was made by God, and don't forget a King's kid.

I took a step with new strength I'd never felt before,
I kissed my comfort zone "goodbye" and closed that stagnant door.

If you are in a comfort zone and afraid to venture out,

Listen to your heart, because there's a fire that needs to be let out.

Remember,

All winners at one time were filled with doubt,
they just made up their mind that they were stepping out.

If you put your mind to it, go after your destiny fearless, and believe it is true,

Guess what?

Success is waiting for you!

"All the comfort in the world couldn't take away my hunger for purpose. I feel like if I don't step out on water, my boat will eventually sink anyway. So, I picked up the pen in my heart, and started to write the words he gave me."

Follow your heart my friend and "U" –turn!

Chapter 18

Eight Steps to Finding Your Passion and Purpose

~

*"Lack of something to feel important about is
almost the greatest tragedy man can have."*

~Arthur E. Morgan

"You can find passion in your pain."

~Terence B. Lester

One of the things that you don't want to do is to go through life with no idea as to what it is that you are really supposed to do. It is good to have both passion and purpose and to figure out as early as possible what both of these are in your life.

Before you identify your ultimate passion, you're probably saying to yourself, "I don't know what I'm supposed to be doing in life." I'm going to give you some simple keys and tips that are helpful in assuring passion and purpose in life. Before the first tip, please take out a notebook, journal, piece of paper, or napkin. These are items you can write on to save your discoveries. These steps will only help you if you pursue them, so, please, either take a moment to find writing tools now or complete this exercise later. It may take you some meditating to get it done.

Here are the eight steps:

1. **<u>Decide what makes you happy.</u>** – Just think about all of the things that you do -- especially the things that you look forward to doing, those things that you would do for free if no one paid you. Make a list of them. Do you get a good feeling? Do you feel good about yourself and what you accomplish during these activities? Do you enjoy the positive comments that people make as a result?

2. **<u>Identify the top items on your list.</u>** – Of all the things that make you happy, identify the top two items. These are the

two things to focus on at present. Remember to have a strategic focus. Because if you focus on too many things, you won't accomplish all that you can.

3. **From these two, what do you do best?** – Now, which one do you do better between the two? Remember to choose the one that makes you the happiest.

4. **How can you perform this activity so well that others will notice what you have done and congratulate you for it?** – Can you think of ways that your contribution will be remembered as the very best? Think about Michael Jordan. Young boys who were not born during his basketball days still recognize him as a basketball superstar. They want his shoes, even though they never really saw him play. He played his very best at all times, and it caused him to stand out. There are some well-known actresses and singers whom young ladies admire as well. Whatever you do well, do it with excellence. Remember, those who go the extra mile stand out. It is the "extra" on the "ordinary" that makes us extraordinary.

5. **Moving forward, find ways to correct past behaviors that might have hurt you or kept you from moving forward.** - If you have to apologize to someone, then now is as good a time as any. It will make you feel good inside, and it will probably cause someone to respect you and look at you in a new light.

6. **Decide if the things that bring you happiness and the things that you do really well present opportunities for progress and success.** - Michael Jordan obviously enjoyed basketball. He also played quite well. This was the perfect combination. But suppose he loved the game, but did not play well? There is something that you do quite well that also provides a real sense of accomplishment. This is not just for young men, but goes for young ladies as well. Do you know of anyone who does something well that brings

them happiness? Find what makes you happy, and do it well.

7. **Develop a plan of action for being the best that you can be, using what you enjoy most and for which you feel the greatest passion.** – Now make a list of the things that you should do to move ahead towards being that best that you can as you enjoy the journey. And, most importantly, start them. Remember, making the list is only half the battle. Many people start things and never finish. You have to make up in your mind to start and follow through with your commitments.

8. **Hang around people who have similar desires.** - This may be the most important of them all. Why? Because you can know what you want to do, do it well, and be happy, but, if you are around the wrong people, there is a strong possibility that you could end up not going as far as you wanted to go. For instance, if your goal is to be a star track runner, you don't want to hang around people who are selling drugs or cutting class. That is a conflict of interest. You want to hang around people who are doing the same things you are doing, so they will keep you motivated and push you to excel. If you are around people who won't push you, you can become lazy and not push yourself. Also, the right people will keep you on track and focused. Always surround yourself with those who have the same passions and are headed somewhere.

Congratulations. You have just created a roadmap for success.

WHAT'S STOPPING YOU?

Chapter 19

Overcomers

~

"Anyone can overcome, if they believe they can overcome."
~Terence B. Lester

I am so grateful that I have lived long enough to see a change in my life. I am happily married, educated, gainfully employed, and well on the way to helping other young people. It has been a tough journey, but I made it. I had a chance to look at what my life might have been if I had not changed some time ago. It all came about during the time that my grandmother (on my mother's side) was ill. She is another individual who prayed for me and tried to keep me on track.

I love her tremendously and did not want to see her suffer. I still remember how she tried to keep me from dropping out of school. She even came over every morning for a long time to carry me to high school just to make sure that I made it there. She tried to get me to show more respect for my mother and to follow the rules of her house while I lived at home.

Anyway, she became ill with a serious condition that required treatment. I went back and forth to the hospital to visit her. She was in one of the best hospitals in Atlanta. It is a teaching hospital and specializes in handling severe conditions. It also attracts all kinds of people — rich, poor, prominent, and just common folk. As I went through the process of going in to see her, I witnessed many scenarios. There were homeless people who gathered outside to panhandle those entering the facility. There were crack heads using crack right there on the premises. There were people totally out of their minds doing all kinds of crazy things. Among the saddest were the working people who showed no signs of being on drugs; neither were they homeless. However, they seemed to have the same countenance of a person who had never really lived. They appeared spiritually and emotionally lifeless.

As I moved among them, through parking lots, into the building, and up elevators, I saw life as God had shown me before.

The thing that was different at this point was that I was determined to help to make a change. Except for the marvelous and protective grace of God, I could have been the crack addict, the homeless person, or the person going through the motions of everyday life with no joy. Even though I had gone through some rough moments, He had lifted me out of a terrible ditch and placed me on the right path. I thought about this as I passed all of these people between the parking lot and the entrance to the hospital. When I would arrive in my grandmother's room, she would greet me and begin to sing the praises of the God I had finally come to love and serve in a real way.

God has a wide-open field in which we are called to work. However, the sincere and dedicated laborers are too few. There are not nearly enough individuals who are willing to reach back and help others who are struggling with life. Many other people saw these troubled individuals outside of the hospital. Not enough of them really cared or gave any consideration as to what they could do to help. I cannot thank Him enough for making me an "overcomer."

I am so grateful for a second chance that I am honored to do my part. I have a hunger and a thirst to see change, not just in the people outside the hospital, but also in you, your friends, family, and community. It starts with you.

I want you all to know that though we may question our individual destinies at times, there are people out there who have never imagined having a destiny at all. That is far too sad for me to ignore.

I looked at my precious grandmother in a hospital bed still willing to testify of God's goodness. I was so glad that she had lived to see her prayers answered where I am concerned. She remains one of my greatest encouragers. The least that I can do is to try to help someone else.

I work with young people on a daily basis who are like those described in an earlier chapter in this book: about to burst. I work hard to win their confidence, to listen to what it is they have to say and offer them words of advice. I started an organization called "The Trailblazer Group" to provide a place for them to be involved in positive and productive activity. Many of them have thanked me for this opportunity. It gave them something to belong to other than a gang.

I tell them about other individuals — some they have heard of and read about and others with whom they may not be familiar. What I emphasize in presenting these individuals is that they have all faced defeat in one way or another. Some grew up in the projects or other public housing, dropped out of school, came from single-parent households, or became drug dealers, pimps, or worse. Others were not involved in criminal activity, but had a lot to face in life before they came to be known as successful. At some point, they made a "U-turn," and that is all that matters. It is really easy to find out the history and background of celebrities and see how they overcame obstacles. I went online to wikipedia.com to research individuals who are well known to find out what they have overcome. I challenge you to research those whom you admire and to read their stories.

Some of the individuals whom I speak about:

Tyler Perry

Before:
Wikipedia says that Tyler Perry was born on September 13, 1969. He was born in Harvey, Louisiana, one of four children. It has been said that his father was a carpenter and his mother worked at the New Orleans Jewish Community Center for most of her life. As Perry grew up, his childhood contained a lot poverty and physical abuse. He was once homeless and lived in his car for three months. Although Perry faced a lot of opposition coming up, he did not allow his circumstances dictate his future. Tyler Perry is a Christian, and still has a strong passion for God.

After:
Wikipedia says that in 1992, while watching an *Oprah Winfrey* show, Perry made up in his mind that he was going to overcome. He had an awakening. He took the advice that it can be restoring to put feelings down on paper, which inspired him to write letters of his painful childhood. These letters eventually became his plays. Perry's first foray into writing was in 1992, when he began writing

a journal, in part to cope with the repercussions of abuse. He developed different characters to voice different ideas in the journal. This work eventually became the musical *I Know I've Been Changed*, about adult survivors of child abuse.

Perry moved to Atlanta in 1992 and worked in a restaurant and as a used car salesman. He managed to save up $12,000 to stage his first play. It was not a success, and over the next six years, he struggled, living in Atlanta. But he persevered until the play finally had a successful run in 1998, first at the House of Blues and later at the Fox Theatre. His following play, a staging of Bishop T. D. Jakes' book *Woman Thou Art Loosed*, was an immediate hit, grossing over $5 million in five months. A film version was later created, starring Kimberly Elise and Cicely Tyson, and was released in theaters on October 1, 2004.

Perry, whose work is aimed at a primarily African-American audience, ultimately created a successful touring theater company. Recordings of some plays were subsequently sold on video and DVD. As of March 2005, Perry's plays had grossed over $75 million in ticket and DVD sales. Today, Tyler Perry is one of America's leading film directors.

Bill Cosby

Before:
Things have not always been so easy for this famous individual. Before the world had a chance to admire and laugh with his television family, he had already experienced a great deal of sacrifice and hard times. He was always smart, but enjoyed clowning around. He was involved in a lot of activities at school and worked before and after school. This caused his grades to suffer in the academically challenging magnet school he attended. He transferred to another school, but still failed the tenth grade. He decided not to go through tenth grade again and got a job as an apprentice in a shoe repair shop. This wasn't challenging enough for him, so he joined the Navy. It was in the Navy that he discovered his passion. He worked with sailors who required physical therapy after being injured in the Korean War. He discovered that there was a great need for education.

After:

Cosby obtained an equivalency diploma through courses in the mail. Next, he won a scholarship to run track. He went to Temple University in Philadelphia and studied physical education for two years. He had not forgotten that he was good at making people laugh, so he found a job working in a bar as a bartender where he kept his customers laughing. Later, he went on stage and made more people laugh. Even though his parents were not happy with the idea, he left college and began a career as a comedian. Years later he received a Bachelor's Degree based on life experience from Temple University.

Cosby and his wife Camille have given millions of dollars to educate young people. He has gone on record, sometimes in the middle of controversy and criticism, with a strong argument for a no-excuse, no-nonsense approach as far as education goes.

Oprah Winfrey

Before:

Oprah was born to unmarried teenagers. Her mother was a housekeeper, and her father worked as a coalminer and later a barber. She was born poor and spent the first years of her life in extreme difficulty. She spent most of her childhood with her grandmother.

At about six years old, she went to live with her mother in the north. Life deteriorated even more, because she did not have the same amount of attention and support that her grandmother had provided. She was a very smart child. At about nine years old, she was molested.

Because she was so smart, Oprah received a scholarship to a very good school. The problem was that most of the students there were quite well off, and she felt like an outsider. This led to all kinds of trouble, including rebellion. Eventually, she ran away from home. By fourteen years old, she was pregnant. The baby died soon after birth. Communication was not that good between her and her mother, so her mother decided to send her to Nashville to live with her father. Her father did not play. He made her get her act together. She made the honor roll and won a scholarship to Tennessee State University, where she studied communication.

131

After:

Oprah is the wealthiest black woman in the world. She is also one of the richest persons, black or white, in America. She has one of the most successful television shows in the United States and owns her own production company. She publishes one of the largest circulated magazines in history. She has successfully acted in movies, launched one of the country's most celebrated book clubs, and, most recently, opened a school for poor girls in Africa. Before this latest contribution to education, she entered into an agreement with Morehouse College in Atlanta, Georgia to send one hundred black men through college.

Fantasia Barrino

Before:

Fantasia was the victim of a sexual assault at a young age. She was so embarrassed that she withdrew from high school. She could not handle the shame, the stares, and the gossip. Later on, at age 17, she gave birth to a child out of wedlock. She had a really difficult time trying to take care of a child at such a young age. She did not have a high school education and did not qualify for a really good job. Both of her parents were performers and traveled throughout the Carolinas doing concerts. Her grandmother was also a pastor of a church.

After:

Although she lacked confidence to the point that she was afraid to risk being turned down during the auditions for the show, she tried out for *American Idol*. Something deep inside gave her the courage to try anyway.

Fantasia gained world recognition as she appeared on the popular show. She made wonderful use of a spectacular voice and an unmistakable church sound that rocked the house week after week. Fantasia got over the shame of being an unwed mother and a high school dropout. She chose not to marry her past and embraced her future. She decided to remember that as a child of God she was entitled to His love, care, and provision. She walked in faith and stood her ground. Thousands of people who never heard of her before began to cast votes in her favor during each show. They did not care about her past. They were excited about her future. Today, she is a much sought-after performer with recording contracts and many concert opportunities. She is able to take care of her daughter and provide the life she always wanted for her.

These are just a few examples of individuals who could have said, "Okay, that's it. I quit." Instead, in the middle of tough times, they discovered passion and moved forward to pursue their dreams. I challenge you to think about my story as well as all of their circumstances and begin that process of turning your life around.

It is now time for your "U-turn." You too are an overcomer.

Chapter 20

What Ya Got?

~

"You have greatness in you, but you'll never know it until you use it."
~Terence B. Lester

This chapter's title is certainly not good English; however, it makes my point. In the Bible there was a man whose name was Moses. God selected him for a very important job. Moses had difficulty speaking and thought that he needed to warn God that he might not be the best man for the job. He also said that he was not well equipped to carry out such a big project. When Moses heard that he would be in the wilderness with millions of people, I bet he started thinking about all kinds of things -- equipment, food, shelter, water, animals, sickness, childbirths, deaths, and a little of everything else.

When he tried to "help God figure it out," God asked a simple question, "What is that in your hand?" You see, Moses had a staff (a long stick) that he carried around. It was his only tool. Since that was all that he had, God worked miracles to make it enough. He held it out at the seashore and divided the Red Sea. At another time, he threw it on the ground, and it turned into a large snake. If you are not real comfortable reading the Bible, just go and find a Bible story-book and follow this amazing story.

I shared the information about Moses, because I want you to think about what it is that you have already that can be used to help you to accomplish your goals. For example, my teacher saw that I liked to write. He encouraged me to do just that. His faith in my ability in that area has helped me to be a published author.

When I think about the world of hip hop music, I often think about how gifted we are and how much we can accomplish through this one type of music because of its appeal to the younger generation. Please allow me to share my thoughts on what could be.

Most Americans do not consider rap worthwhile. Many people turn up their noses when they hear the word. However, rap is an

American form of music created primarily by urban artists who happen to be black. It has been around for over twenty years and is alive and well. In other words, it isn't going anywhere. It is here to stay. Some people credit the Bronx in New York as the birthplace of hip hop culture, as it provided an excellent place for rap music to begin. In actuality, as we hear it today, there are influences from a lot of places in modern rap music, including places as far away as Jamaica and Europe.

If people understood how music is made, they might be a little more receptive to rap and its message. It is definitely an urban (city) kind of musical contribution. Often it deals with life issues, government, war, poverty, family matters, and a little of everything else.

In Steven Hager's book, *Hip Hop: the Illustrated History of Break Dancing, Rap Music and Graffiti*, three major events shaped the beginning of hip hop and rap music:

- In 1959, there was an expressway built straight through the heart of the Bronx in New York. When this happened, many of the ethnic groups (middle-class Italians, Germans, Irish and Jewish) moved away. Then many businesses left this area (borough) of New York. When the businesses and middle class homes became vacant, the communities became largely black and Hispanic.
- In 1968, there was a major building project that involved adding over 15,000 apartments in the Bronx area near the expressway. The few middle-class people who remained in the Bronx moved away because they did not want to live near this large apartment complex.
- About the same time (1968), gang activity began to grow faster than ever in New York.

It would seem as though nothing good could come from the circumstances listed above; however, over the course of years, rap music became an outlet to "rhyme" about changing neighborhoods, conditions in the street, needless death, male/female relationships, and a lot of other life issues. The first rap records to make the charts big time were "Rapper's Delight," by the Sugar Hill Gang,

"White Lines," a rap about not using drugs, and "The Message," a rap about life in Black America. For a long time, rap music was created by blacks for blacks. Later on, Run-D.M.C. became the first group to break the racial barrier by selling in mass to white listening audiences. They were actually not your typical rap artists, because they were middle-class themselves. They simply hopped on to "what was hot."

I went through all of that history just to share how people can use their surroundings and circumstances to build something good or bad. There are rappers who once produced very negative lyrics who have switched to a positive message. Percy Robert Miller, known in the music industry as Master P, is just one example. Christian bookstores have many examples of great rap artists who perform only Christian lyrics.

Our communities are still filled with problems but you have the power and the ability to create a positive message and "get it out there." If you really enjoy rap and writing down what you feel, why not write good stuff, get on the "open mic" circuit, and do something that will make a better person of you and someone else as well? You have influence. Someone will listen.

Maybe you are a talented athlete. Why not use your ability to be great in the life of a child younger than you who might look up to you at your games? Are you a cheerleader? Why not create cheers that will help little children learn the continents, multiplication tables, parts of speech, and a lot more?

Do you put your clothes together well? Can you put outfits on and look like a million dollars even if you only spent $20.00? Then why not start designing your own line? Why not go ahead and make sketches? Why not create a portfolio? Can you really clean a house? Why not begin to learn to do a business plan so that you can have your own cleaning service? Can you make people laugh? Can you make up a joke with no problem at all? Well, guess what? Eddie Murphy and Chris Rock had the very same gift. Look where they are today.

If you stand before God and tell him what you can't do and that you have nothing to do it with, He will eventually bring someone in your path to show you exactly how well He has equipped you.

Chapter 21

Go For It

~

Dear Reader,

Now that you have just finished this book, I am writing a letter especially for you. I want you to know that no matter where you are, what you have, or whom you are around in life, you are a special person and have greatness inside you. It doesn't matter if you feel as if you are not the smartest or if you feel that you're not the most popular person. All that matters is that you believe in yourself. I want you to know that there is really a treasure inside of you, and to discover it, all you have to do is make up in your mind that from this day forward you will commit yourself and promise God that you will move forward.

I also want to encourage you that whatever dreams you have, they are attainable if you believe in yourself. I want you to understand that everything always starts with a belief, and that's why, if you believe that you can change your life, you can, if you start now and leave out all blame and excuses. It may not happen overnight, but as you are consistent you will have a reward that no one will ever be able to take from you. I want you to know that I believe in you wholeheartedly and believe that you can do it. I believe that you are an overcomer and that you will go very far in life, despite what trials you may have gone through. You have to keep reminding yourself everyday: "I can make it."

As you wrap up this book, I encourage you to "go for it." Go for your dreams, go for changing your life around, go for helping your mother or father around the house, go for being the best you that you can possibly be. Henry Ford, the founder of Ford Motors, said something that I'll never forget. He said, "If you think you can, or if you think you can't, either way, you're right." That statement alone gives us the power to achieve or to stay where we are.

I want you to know that you have the power to change how you react to what happens to you. One thing that I learned coming up is that plenty of people start things, but few actually follow through. It takes a leader like you to start and finish. That is simply saying, put application to whatever you learn that can benefit you.

Please allow me to close with this. From this day forward, try something you've never tried that's positive: read a book that you've never read, expose yourself to new things that could possibly benefit your life, dream big, and always believe in yourself. I want you to know that you are on the way to greatness if you believe and continue to grow. Now, "Go for it!"

Your Friend,
Terence B. Lester
terencelester.com

ABOUT THE AUTHOR

~

Terence B. Lester was born in Atlanta, GA on December 4th, 1982. He is the son of Tyrone Lester and Connie Walker and has one younger sister; Ashley Lester. He has a wonderful supporting wife, Cecilia L. Lester who aids him with his speaking and writing. His life is dedicated to mentoring young people as they are forced to make tough decisions in a difficult world. Although only 24 years old, this young man has lived through peril, trial, disappointment and now---jubilation! He emerges as a powerful and dynamic spokesperson ably equipped to address an entire generation. Unfortunately, the voices of parents often go unheard. Their repeated message becomes constant. Their pleas for conformity often fall on deaf ears. Lester serves as a willing Christian Mediator. He is for BOTH sides. He understands misguided youth and he empathizes with troubled parents. According to this high-energy crusader, "There IS an oasis in the middle of this wilderness experience!"

With fresh memories of a turbulent childhood, he is destined to help young people avoid traps that become deadly as each day goes by. His goal is to bring young people and their parents to a meaningful point of understanding and agreement. Though it sounds like an impossible dream, it has become reality for Terence, his mother, his wife and those who prayed for him over many years. Now he is a much sought-after speaker and facilitator of youth group sessions and conferences. He is also a recognized poet and a prolific writer. A devout Christian and follower of Jesus Christ, Lester reminds the world that there is absolutely NOTHING too hard for God! Since God has planted a burning desire to lead young people out of a modern-day Egypt, he has no doubt that the same God will prove faithful and use him to continue to share a message of love, hope, reconciliation, healing and divine destiny to thousands. Equipped with prayer and an unusual ability to relate to his audience, Lester stands boldly before young people not as another religious leader but as a child of God with a fresh application and covering of the blood of Jesus each time he addresses a group. It takes only moments for them to realize that this young man is FOR REAL!

Lester comes not to challenge prior Christian teaching or diminish parental influence. Rather, he comes to augment and make plain that which has been spoken. Until the message is understood, and until it has been received, it may as well not have been delivered at all. He has come to stand in partnership and agreement with those who love God and are unwilling to give up on young people. Our youth DESERVE the chance to sit at the feet of an ex-juvenile delinquent, an ex-drug user, a former thief, an ex-gang member and a defiant son. They deserve the chance to see what God has done in his life. They will have to see the changed man to believe it. They need to meet and touch a man who has definitely made a "U Turn."

Prepare to receive letters of testimony and thanks after this young man has had the opportunity to minister to a confused generation wandering in an even more confused world. If you have been praying to God for ways to spiritually impact your young people, son, daughter or one young person in particular, then Terence B. Lester is a part of your answer.

Hear ye Him!

CONTACT INFORMATION

~

Terence Lester is available for speaking engagements, book signings, workshops, and conference participation. Please submit details to the following address:

Terence Lester
PO BOX 43383
Atlanta, GA, 30336

To book engagements, please send:

- Date and length of event
- Contact person
- Contact information (phone, fax, email address)
- Event type (Conference, ministry engagement-church service, youth service, panel participant, etc.)
- Target audience (church congregation, mixed ages, youth service, young adults, etc.)
- Venue and size of engagement

You may go online and request Terence Lester's services or books on the World Wide Web.

Website:
www.terencelester.com

Email Address:
contact@terencelester.com

Phone:
404-606-3116
770-875-3462

Thanks for your support!

Made in the USA